The Jero Plays

This volume contains two short plays about Brother Jeroboam, the rather less than holy West African 'beach divine' created by the Nigerian playwright Wole Soyinka. In the original comedy *The Trials of Brother Jero*, first published in 1964, the charlatan preacher, burdened by a cross 'daughter of Eve', uses Christian superstition for his own salvation. In the new sequel, *Jero's Metamorphosis*, the profit-minded 'prophet' thwarts a government attempt to cleanse the beach of all the dubious brethren who ply their trade there.

The photograph on the front of the cover shows a scene from the Ijinle Theatre production of The Trials of Brother Jero *at the Hampstead Theatre Club; this photograph and the photograph of Wole Soyinka on the back of the cover are reproduced by courtesy of John Goldblatt.*

Wole Soyinka

THE JERO PLAYS

METHUEN LONDON

The Trials of Brother Jero *first published in Great Britain
in 1964 by Oxford University Press*
Jero's Metamorphosis *first published in Great Britain
1973 by Eyre Methuen Ltd
11 New Fetter Lane, London EC4P 4EE*
The Trials of Brother Jero *and*
Jero's Metamorphosis
reprinted 1977, 1978 (twice), 1979, 1981 and 1986
The Trials of Brother Jero © *1964 and 1973
by Wole Soyinka*
Jero's Metamorphosis © *1973 by Wole Soyinka*

ISBN 0 413 29230 4 (Hardback)
ISBN 0 413 29240 1 (Paperback)

*Printed and bound in Great Britain by
Richard Clay Ltd, Bungay, Suffolk*

Contents

THE TRIALS
OF BROTHER JERO

CAST

JEROBOAM, *a Beach Divine*
OLD PROPHET, *his mentor*
CHUME, *assistant to Jeroboam*
AMOPE, *his wife*
A TRADER
MEMBER OF PARLIAMENT
THE PENITENT, *a woman*
THE ANGRY WOMAN, *a tough mamma*
A YOUNG GIRL
A DRUMMER BOY
A MAN AND AN OLD COUPLE (*worshippers*)

SCENE ONE

The stage is completely dark. A spotlight reveals the PROPHET, *a heavily but neatly bearded man; his hair is thick and high, but well-combed, unlike that of most prophets. Suave is the word for him. He carries a canvas pouch and a divine rod.* He speaks directly and with his accustomed loftiness to the audience.*

JERO. I am a prophet. A prophet by birth and by inclination. You have probably seen many of us on the streets, many with their own churches, many inland, many on the coast, many leading processions, many looking for processions to lead, many curing the deaf, many raising the dead. In fact, there are eggs and there are eggs. Same thing with prophets. I was born a prophet. I think my parents found that I was born with rather thick and long hair. It was said to come right down to my eyes and down to my neck. For them, this was a certain sign that I was born a natural prophet. And I grew to love the trade. It used to be a very respectable one in those days and competition was dignified. But in the last few years, the beach has become fashionable, and the struggle for land has turned the profession into a thing of ridicule. Some prophets I could name gained their present beaches by getting women penitents to shake their bosoms in spiritual ecstasy. This prejudiced the councillors who came to divide the beach among us. Yes, it did come to the point where it became necessary for the Town Council to come to the beach and settle the prophets' territorial warfare once and for all. My Master, the same one who brought me up

* A metal rod about eighteen inches long, tapered, bent into a ring at the thick end.

in prophetic ways staked his claim and won a grant of land . . . I helped him, with a campaign led by six dancing girls from the French territory, all dressed as Jehovah's Witnesses. What my old Master did not realize was that I was really helping myself. Mind you, the beach is hardly worth having these days. The worshippers have dwindled to a mere trickle and we really have to fight for every new convert. They all prefer High Life to the rhythm of celestial hymns. And television too is keeping our wealthier patrons at home. They used to come in the evening when they would not easily be recognized. Now they stay at home and watch television. However, my whole purpose in coming here is to show you one rather eventful day in my life, a day when I thought for a moment that the curse of my old Master was about to be fulfilled. It shook me quite a bit, but . . . the Lord protects his own . . .

Enter OLD PROPHET *shaking his fist.*

OLD PROPHET. Ungrateful wretch! Is this how you repay the long years of training I have given you? To drive me, your old Tutor, off my piece of land . . . telling me I have lived beyond my time. Ha! May you be rewarded in the same manner. May the wheel come right round and find you just as helpless as you make me now . . .

He continues to mouth curses, but inaudibly.

JERO (*ignoring him*). He didn't move me one bit. The old dodderer had been foolish enough to imagine that when I organized the campaign to acquire his land in competition with (*Ticking them off on his fingers.*) – The Brotherhood of Jehu, the Cherubims and Seraphims, the Sisters of Judgement Day, the Heavenly Cowboys, not to mention the Jehovah's Witnesses whom the French girls impersonated – well, he must have been pretty conceited to think that I did it all for him.

OLD PROPHET. Ingrate! Monster! I curse you with the curse of the Daughters of Discord. May they be your downfall. May the Daughters of Eve bring ruin down on your head!

OLD PROPHET *goes off, shaking his fist.*

JERO. Actually that was a very cheap curse. He knew very well that I had one weakness – women. Not my fault, mind you. You must admit that I am rather good-looking . . . no, don't be misled, I am not at all vain. Nevertheless, I decided to be on my guard. The call of prophecy is in my blood and I would not risk my calling with the fickleness of women. So I kept away from them. I am still single and since that day when I came into my own, no scandal has ever touched my name. And it was a sad day indeed when I woke up one morning and the first thing to meet my eyes was a daughter of Eve. You may compare that feeling with waking up and finding a vulture crouched on your bedpost.

Blackout.

SCENE TWO

Early morning.

A few poles with nets and other litter denote a fishing village. Downstage right is the corner of a hut, window on one side, door on the other.

A cycle bell is heard ringing. Seconds after, a cycle is ridden on stage towards the hut. The rider is a shortish man; his feet barely touch the pedals. On the cross-bar is a woman; the cross-bar itself is wound

*round with a mat, and on the carrier is a large travelling sack, with
a woman's household stool hanging from a corner of it.*

AMOPE. Stop here. Stop here. That's his house.

> *The man applies the brakes too suddenly. The weight leans
> towards the woman's side, with the result that she props up the
> bicycle with her feet, rather jerkily. It is in fact no worse than
> any ordinary landing, but it is enough to bring out her sense of
> aggrievement.*

AMOPE (*her tone of martyrdom is easy, accustomed to use*). I suppose
we all do our best, but after all these years one would think you
could set me down a little more gently.

CHUME. You didn't give me much notice. I had to brake suddenly.

AMOPE. The way you complain – anybody who didn't see what
happened would think you were the one who broke an ankle.
(*She has already begun to limp.*)

CHUME. Don't tell me that was enough to break your ankle.

AMOPE. Break? You didn't hear me complain. You did your best,
but if my toes are to be broken one by one just because I have to
monkey on your bicycle, you must admit it's a tough life for a
woman.

CHUME. I did my . . .

AMOPE. Yes, you did your best. I know. Didn't I admit it? Please
. . . give me that stool . . . You know yourself that I'm not the
one to make much of a little thing like that, but I haven't been
too well. If anyone knows that, it's you. Thank you (*Taking the
stool.*) . . . I haven't been well, that's all. Otherwise I wouldn't
have said a thing.

> *She sits down near the door of the hut, sighing heavily, and
> begins to nurse her feet.*

CHUME. Do you want me to bandage it for you?

AMOPE. No, no. What for?

CHUME *hesitates, then begins to unload the bundle.*

CHUME. You're sure you don't want me to take you back? If it swells after I've gone . . .

AMOPE. I can look after myself. I've always done, and looked after you too. Just help me unload the things and place them against the wall . . . you know I wouldn't ask if it wasn't for the ankle.

CHUME *had placed the bag next to her, thinking that was all. He returns now to unpack the bundle. Brings out a small brazier covered with paper which is tied down, two small saucepans . . .*

AMOPE. You haven't let the soup pour out, have you?

CHUME (*with some show of exasperation*). Do you see oil on the wrapper? (*Throws down the wrapper.*)

AMOPE. Abuse me. All right, go on, begin to abuse me. You know that all I asked was if the soup had poured away, and it isn't as if that was something no one ever asked before. I would do it all myself if it wasn't for my ankle – anyone would think it was my fault . . . careful . . . careful now . . . the cork nearly came off that bottle. You know how difficult it is to get any clean water in this place . . .

CHUME *unloads two bottles filled with water, two little parcels wrapped in paper, another tied in a knot, a box of matches, a piece of yam, two tins, one probably an Ovaltine tin but containing something else of course, a cheap breakable spoon, a knife, while* AMOPE *keeps up her patient monologue, spoken almost with indifference.*

AMOPE. Do, I beg you, take better care of that jar . . . I know you didn't want to bring me, but it wasn't the fault of the jar, was it?

CHUME. Who said I didn't want to bring you?

AMOPE. You said it was too far away for you to bring me on your bicycle . . . I suppose you really wanted me to walk . . .

CHUME. I . . .

AMOPE. And after you'd broken my foot, the first thing you asked was if you should take me home. You were only too glad it happened . . . in fact if I wasn't the kind of person who would never think evil of anyone – even you – I would have said that you did it on purpose.

The unloading is over. CHUME *shakes out the bag.*

AMOPE. Just leave the bag here. I can use it for a pillow.

CHUME. Is there anything else before I go?

AMOPE. You've forgotten the mat. I know it's not much, but I would like something to sleep on. There are women who sleep in beds of course, but I'm not complaining . . . They are just lucky with their husbands, and we can't all be lucky I suppose.

CHUME. You've got a bed at home.

He unties the mat which is wound round the cross-bar.

AMOPE. And so I'm to leave my work undone. My trade is to suffer because I have a bed at home? Thank God I am not the kind of woman who . . .

CHUME. I am nearly late for work.

AMOPE. I know you can't wait to get away. You only use your work as an excuse. A Chief Messenger in the Local Government Office – do you call that work? Your old school friends are now Ministers, riding in long cars . . .

CHUME *gets on his bike and flees.* AMOPE *shouts after him, craning her neck in his direction.*

AMOPE. Don't forget to bring some more water when you're

returning from work. (*She relapses and sighs heavily.*) He doesn't realize it is all for his own good. He's no worse than other men, but he won't make the effort to become something in life. A Chief Messenger. Am I to go to my grave as the wife of a Chief Messenger?

She is seated so that the PROPHET *does not immediately see her when he opens the window to breathe some fresh air. He stares straight out for a few moments, then shuts his eyes tightly, clasps his hands together above his chest, chin uplifted for a few moments' meditation. He relaxes and is about to go in when he sees* AMOPE's *back. He leans out to try and take in the rest of her, but this proves impossible. Puzzled, he leaves the window and goes round to the door which is then seen to open about a foot and shut rapidly.*

AMOPE *is calmly chewing kola. As the door shuts she takes out a notebook and a pencil and checks some figures.*

PROPHET JEROBOAM, *known to his congregation as* BROTHER JERO, *is seen again at the window, this time with his canvas pouch and divine stick. He lowers the bag to the ground, eases one leg over the window.*

AMOPE (*without looking back*). Where do you think you're going?

BROTHER JERO *practically flings himself back into the house.*

AMOPE. One pound, eight shillings and ninepence for three months. And he calls himself a man of God.

She puts the notebook away, unwraps the brazier and proceeds to light it preparatory to getting breakfast.
The door opens another foot.

JERO (*coughs*). Sister . . . my dear sister in Christ . . .
AMOPE. I hope you slept well, Brother Jero . . .

JERO. Yes, thanks be to God. (*Hems and coughs.*) I – er – I hope you have not come to stand in the way of Christ and his work.

AMOPE. If Christ doesn't stand in the way of me and my work.

JERO. Beware of pride, sister. That was a sinful way to talk.

AMOPE. Listen, you bearded debtor. You owe me one pound, eight and nine. You promised you would pay me three months ago but of course you have been too busy doing the work of God. Well, let me tell you that you are not going anywhere until you do a bit of my own work.

JERO. But the money is not in the house. I must get it from the post office before I can pay you.

AMOPE (*fanning the brazier*). You'll have to think of something else before you call me a fool.

> BROTHER JEROBOAM *shuts the door.*
> A woman TRADER *goes past with a deep calabash bowl on her head.*

AMOPE. Ei, what are you selling?

> *The* TRADER *hesitates, decides to continue on her way.*

AMOPE. Isn't it you I'm calling? What have you got there?

TRADER (*stops without turning round*). Are you buying for trade or just for yourself?

AMOPE. It might help if you first told me what you have.

TRADER. Smoked fish.

AMOPE. Well, let's see it.

TRADER (*hesitates*). All right, help me to set it down. But I don't usually stop on the way.

AMOPE. Isn't it money you are going to the market for, and isn't it money I'm going to pay you?

TRADER (*as* AMOPE *gets up and unloads her*). Well, just remember it is early in the morning. Don't start me off wrong by haggling.

AMOPE. All right, all right. (*Looks at the fish.*) How much a dozen?

TRADER. One and three, and I'm not taking a penny less.

AMOPE. It is last week's, isn't it?

TRADER. I've told you, you're my first customer, so don't ruin my trade with the ill-luck of the morning.

AMOPE (*holding one up to her nose*). Well, it does smell a bit, doesn't it?

TRADER (*putting back the wrappings*). Maybe it is you who haven't had a bath for a week.

AMOPE. Yeh! All right, go on. Abuse me. Go on and abuse me when all I wanted was a few of your miserable fish. I deserve it for trying to be neighbourly with a cross-eyed wretch, pauper that you are . . .

TRADER. It is early in the morning. I am not going to let you infect my luck with your foul tongue by answering you back. And just you keep your cursed fingers from my goods because that is where you'll meet with the father of all devils if you don't.

She lifts the load to her head all by herself.

AMOPE. Yes, go on. Carry the burden of your crimes and take your beggar's rags out of my sight . . .

TRADER. I leave you in the hands of your flatulent belly, you barren sinner. May you never do good in all your life.

AMOPE. You're cursing me now, are you?

She leaps up just in time to see BROTHER JERO *escape through the window.*

Help! Thief! Thief! You bearded rogue. Call yourself a prophet? But you'll find it is easier to get out than to get in. You'll find that out or my name isn't Amope . . .

She turns on the TRADER *who has already disappeared.*

Do you see what you have done, you spindle-leg toad? Receiver of stolen goods, just wait until the police catch up with you . . .

Towards the end of this speech the sound of gangan drums is heard, coming from the side opposite the hut. A BOY *enters carrying a drum on each shoulder. He walks towards her, drumming. She turns almost at once.*

AMOPE. Take yourself off, you dirty beggar. Do you think my money is for the likes of you?

The BOY *flees, turns suddenly and beats a parting abuse on the drums.**

AMOPE. I don't know what the world is coming to. A thief of a prophet, a swindler of a fish-seller and now that thing with lice on his head comes begging for money. He and the prophet ought to get together with the fish-seller their mother.

Lights fade.

SCENE THREE

A short while later. The Beach. A few stakes and palm leaves denote the territory of Brother Jeroboam's church. To one side is a palm tree, and in the centre is a heap of sand with assorted empty bottles, a small mirror, and hanging from one of the bottles is a rosary and cross. BROTHER JERO *is standing as he was last seen when he made his escape – white flowing gown and a very fine velvet cape, white also.*

* Urchins often go through the streets with a drum, begging for alms. But their skill is used also for insults even without provocation.

Stands upright, divine rod in hand, while the other caresses the velvet cape.

JERO. I don't know how she found out my house. When I bought the goods off her, she did not even ask any questions. My calling was enough to guarantee payment. It is not as if this was a well-paid job. And it is not what I would call a luxury, this velvet cape which I bought from her. It would not have been necessary if one were not forced to distinguish himself more and more from these scum who degrade the calling of the prophet. It becomes important to stand out, to be distinctive. I have set my heart after a particular name. They will look at my velvet cape and they will think of my goodness. Inevitably they must begin to call me . . . the Velvet-hearted Jeroboam. (*Straightens himself.*) Immaculate Jero, Articulate Hero of Christ's Crusade . . . Well, it is out. I have not breathed it to a single soul, but that has been my ambition. You've got to have a name that appeals to the imagination – because the imagination is a thing of the spirit – it must catch the imagination of the crowd. Yes, one must move with modern times. Lack of colour gets one nowhere even in the prophet's business.

Looks all round him.

Charlatans! If only I had this beach to myself. (*With sudden violence.*) But how does one maintain his dignity when the daughter of Eve forces him to leave his own house through a window? God curse that woman! I never thought she would dare affront the presence of a man of God. One pound eight for this little cape. It is sheer robbery.

He surveys the scene again. A YOUNG GIRL *passes, sleepily, clothed only in her wrapper.*

JERO. She passes here every morning, on her way to take a swim. Dirty-looking thing.

He yawns.

I am glad I got here before any customers – I mean worshippers – well, customers if you like. I always get that feeling every morning that I am a shop-keeper waiting for customers. The regular ones come at definite times. Strange, dissatisfied people. I know they are dissatisfied because I keep them dissatisfied. Once they are full, they won't come again. Like my good apprentice, Brother Chume. He wants to beat his wife, but I won't let him. If I do, he will become contented, and then that's another of my flock gone for ever. As long as he doesn't beat her, he comes here feeling helpless, and so there is no chance of his rebelling against me. Everything, in fact, is planned.

The YOUNG GIRL *crosses the stage again. She has just had her swim and the difference is remarkable. Clean, wet, shiny face and hair. She continues to wipe herself with her wrapper as she walks.*

JERO (*following her all the way with his eyes*). Every morning, every day I witness this divine transformation, O Lord.

He shakes his head suddenly and bellows.

Pray Brother Jeroboam, pray! Pray for strength against temptation.

He falls on his knees, face squeezed in agony and hands clasped. CHUME *enters, wheeling his bike. He leans it against the palm tree.*

JERO (*not opening his eyes*). Pray with me, brother. Pray with me. Pray for me against this one weakness ... against this one weakness, O Lord ...

CHUME (*falling down at once*). Help him, Lord. Help him, Lord.

JERO. Against this one weakness, this weakness, O Abraham ...

CHUME. Help him, Lord. Help him, Lord.

JERO. Against this one weakness David, David, Samuel, Samuel.

CHUME. Help him. Help him. Help 'am. Help 'am.

JERO. Job Job, Elijah Elijah.

CHUME (*getting more worked up*). Help 'am God. Help' am God. I say make you help 'am. Help 'am quick quick.

JERO. Tear the image from my heart. Tear this love for the daughters of Eve ...

CHUME. Adam, help 'am. Na your son, help 'am. Help this your son.

JERO. Burn out this lust for the daughters of Eve.

CHUME. Je-e-esu, J-e-esu, Je-e-esu. Help 'am one time Je-e-e-e-su.

JERO. Abraka, Abraka, Abraka.

   CHUME *joins in.*

Abraka, Abraka, Hebra, Hebra, Hebra, Hebra, Hebra, Hebra, Hebra, Hebra ...

JERO (*rising*). God bless you, brother. (*Turns around.*) Chume!

CHUME. Good morning, Brother Jeroboam.

JERO. Chume, you are not at work. You've never come before in the morning.

CHUME. No. I went to work but I had to report sick.

JERO. Why, are you unwell, brother?

CHUME. No, Brother Jero ... I ...

JERO. A-ah, you have troubles and you could not wait to get them to God. We shall pray together.

CHUME. Brother Jero ... I ... I. (*He stops altogether.*)

JERO. Is it difficult? Then let us commune silently for a while.

   CHUME *folds his arms, raises his eyes to heaven.*

JERO. I wonder what is the matter with him. Actually I knew it was he the moment he opened his mouth. Only Brother Chume reverts to that animal jabber when he gets his spiritual excitement. And that is much too often for my liking. He is too crude, but then that is to my advantage. It means he would never think of setting himself up as my equal.

He joins CHUME *in his meditative attitude, but almost immediately discards it, as if he has just remembered something.*

Christ my Protector! It is a good job I got away from that wretched woman as soon as I did. My disciple believes that I sleep on the beach, that is, if he thinks I sleep at all. Most of them believe the same, but, for myself, I prefer my bed. Much more comfortable. And it gets rather cold on the beach at nights. Still, it does them good to believe that I am something of an ascetic . . .

He resumes his meditative pose for a couple of moments.

(*Gently.*) Open your mind to God, brother. This is the tabernacle of Christ. Open your mind to God.

CHUME *is silent for a while, then bursts out suddenly.*

CHUME. Brother Jero, you must let me beat her!
JERO. What!
CHUME (*desperately*). Just once, Prophet. Just once.
JERO. Brother Chume!
CHUME. Just once. Just one sound beating, and I swear not to ask again.
JERO. Apostate. Have I not told you the will of God in this matter?
CHUME. But I've got to beat her, Prophet. You must save me from madness.

JERO. I will. But only if you obey me.

CHUME. In anything else, Prophet. But for this one, make you let me just beat 'am once.

JERO. Apostate!

CHUME. I no go beat 'am too hard. Jus' once, small small.

JERO. Traitor!

CHUME. Jus' this one time. I no' go ask again. Jus' do me this one favour, make a beat 'am today.

JERO. Brother Chume, what were you before you came to me?

CHUME. Prophet . . .

JERO (*sternly*). What were you before the grace of God?

CHUME. A labourer, Prophet. A common labourer.

JERO. And did I not prophesy you would become an office boy?

CHUME. You do 'am, brother. Na so.

JERO. And then a messenger?

CHUME. Na you do' am, brother, na you.

JERO. And then quick promotion? Did I not prophesy it?

CHUME. Na true, Prophet. Na true.

JERO. And what are you now? What are you?

CHUME. Chief Messenger.

JERO. By the grace of God! And by the grace of God, have I not seen you at the table of the Chief Clerk? And you behind the desk, giving orders?

CHUME. Yes, Prophet . . . but . . .

JERO. With a telephone and a table bell for calling the Messenger?

CHUME. Very true, Prophet, but . . .

JERO. But? But? Kneel! (*Pointing to the ground.*) Kneel!

CHUME (*wringing his hands*). Prophet!

JERO. Kneel, sinner, kneel. Hardener of heart, harbourer of Ashtoreth, Protector of Baal, kneel, kneel.

CHUME *falls on his knees.*

CHUME. My life is a hell . . .

JERO. Forgive him, Father, forgive him.

CHUME. This woman will kill me . . .

JERO. Forgive him, Father, forgive him.

CHUME. Only this morning I . . .

JERO. Forgive him, Father, forgive him.

CHUME. All the way on my bicycle . . .

JERO. Forgive . . .

CHUME. And not a word of thanks . . .

JERO. Out Ashtoreth. Out Baal . . .

CHUME. All she gave me was abuse, abuse, abuse . . .

JERO. Hardener of the heart . . .

CHUME. Nothing but abuse . . .

JERO. Petrifier of the soul . . .

CHUME. If I could only beat her once, only once . . .

JERO (*shouting him down*). Forgive this sinner, Father. Forgive him by day, forgive him by night, forgive him in the morning, forgive him at noon . . .

> *A* MAN *enters. Kneels at once and begins to chorus 'Amen', or 'Forgive him, Lord', or 'In the name of Jesus' (pronounced Je-e-e-sus). Those who follow later do the same.*

. . . This is the son whom you appointed to follow in my footsteps. Soften his heart. Brother Chume, this woman whom you so desire to beat is your cross – bear it well. She is your heaven-sent trial – lay not your hands on her. I command you to speak no harsh word to her. Pray, Brother Chume, for strength in this hour of your trial. Pray for strength and fortitude.

> JEROBOAM *leaves them to continue their chorus,* CHUME *chanting 'Mercy, Mercy' while he makes his next remarks.*

They begin to arrive. As usual in the same order. This one who always comes earliest, I have prophesied that he will be made a chief in his home town. That is a very safe prophecy. As safe as our most popular prophecy, that a man will live to be eighty. If it doesn't come true . . .

Enter an OLD COUPLE, *joining chorus as before.*

that man doesn't find out until he's on the other side. So everybody is quite happy. One of my most faithful adherents – unfortunately, he can only be present at weekends – firmly believes that he is going to be the first Prime Minister of the new Mid-North-East State – when it is created. That was a risky prophecy of mine, but I badly needed more worshippers around that time.

He looks at his watch.

The next one to arrive is my most faithful penitent. She wants children, so she is quite a sad case. Or you would think so. But even in the midst of her most self-abasing convulsions, she manages to notice everything that goes on around her. In fact, I had better get back to the service. She is always the one to tell me that my mind is not on the service . . .

Altering his manner –

Rise, Brother Chume. Rise and let the Lord enter into you. Apprentice of the Lord, are you not he upon whose shoulders my mantle must descend?

A woman (the PENITENT*) enters and kneels at once in an attitude of prayer.*

CHUME. It is so, Brother Jero.
JERO. Then why do you harden your heart? The Lord says that you may not beat the good woman whom he has chosen to be your wife, to be your cross in your period of trial, and will you disobey him?
CHUME. No, Brother Jero.
JERO. Will you?

CHUME. No, Brother Jero.
JERO. Praise be to God.
CONGREGATION. Praise be to God.
JERO. Allelu . . .
CONGREGATION. Alleluia.

> *To the clapping of hands, they sing 'I will follow Jesus', swaying and then dancing as they get warmer.* BROTHER JERO, *as the singing starts, hands two empty bottles to* CHUME *who goes to fill them with water from the sea.* CHUME *has hardly gone out when the* DRUMMER BOY *enters from upstage, running. He is rather weighed down by two gangan drums, and darts fearful glances back in mortal terror of whatever it is that is chasing him. This turns out, some ten or so yards later, to be a* WOMAN, *sash tightened around her waist, wrapper pulled so high up that half the length of her thigh is exposed. Her sleeves are rolled above the shoulder and she is striding after the* DRUMMER *in an unmistakable manner.* JEROBOAM, *who has followed the* WOMAN's *exposed limbs with quite distressed concentration, comes suddenly to himself and kneels sharply, muttering. Again the* DRUMMER *appears, going across the stage in a different direction, running still. The* WOMAN *follows, distance undiminished, the same set pace.* JEROBOAM *calls to him.*

JERO. What did you do to her?
DRUMMER (*without stopping*). Nothing. I was only drumming and then she said I was using it to abuse her father.
JERO (*as the* WOMAN *comes into sight*). Woman!

> *She continues out.* CHUME *enters with filled bottles.*

JERO (*shaking his head*). I know her very well. She's my neighbour. But she ignored me . . .

> JEROBOAM *prepares to bless the water when once again the procession appears,* DRUMMER *first and the* WOMAN *after.*

JERO. Come here. She wouldn't dare touch you.
DRUMMER (*increasing his pace*). You don't know her . . .

The WOMAN *comes in sight.*

JERO. Neighbour, neighbour. My dear sister in Moses . . .

She continues her pursuit off-stage. JERO *hesitates, then hands over his rod to* CHUME *and goes after them.*

CHUME (*suddenly remembering*). You haven't blessed the water, Brother Jeroboam.

JERO is already out of hearing. CHUME *is obviously bewildered by the new responsibility. He fiddles around with the rod and eventually uses it to conduct the singing, which has gone on all this time, flagging when the two contestants came in view, and reviving again after they had passed.*
CHUME *has hardly begun to conduct his band when a woman detaches herself from the crowd in the expected penitent's paroxysm.*

PENITENT. Echa, echa, echa, echa, echa . . . eei, eei, eei, eei.
CHUME (*taken aback*). Ngh? What's the matter?
PENITENT. Efie, efie, efie, efie, enh, enh, enh, enh . . .
CHUME (*dashing off*). Brother Jeroboam, Brother Jeroboam . . .

CHUME shouts in all directions, returning confusedly each time in an attempt to minister to the PENITENT. *As* JEROBOAM *is not forthcoming, he begins very uncertainly, to sprinkle some of the water on the* PENITENT, *crossing her on the forehead. This has to be achieved very rapidly in the brief moment when the* PENITENT'S *head is lifted from beating on the ground.*

CHUME (*stammering*). Father . . . forgive her.

CONGREGATION (*strongly*). Amen.

> *The unexpectedness of the response nearly throws* CHUME, *but then it also serves to bolster him up, receiving such support.*

CHUME. Father, forgive her.
CONGREGATION. Amen.

> *The* PENITENT *continues to moan.*

CHUME. Father, forgive her.
CONGREGATION. Amen.
CHUME. Father, forgive 'am.
CONGREGATION. Amen.
CHUME (*warming up to the task*). Make you forgive 'am. Father.
CONGREGATION. Amen.

> *They rapidly gain pace,* CHUME *getting quite carried away.*

CHUME. I say make you forgive 'am.
CONGREGATION. Amen.
CHUME. Forgive 'am one time.
CONGREGATION. Amen.
CHUME. Forgive 'am quick, quick.
CONGREGATION. Amen.
CHUME. Forgive 'am, Father.
CONGREGATION. Amen.
CHUME. Forgive us all.
CONGREGATION. Amen.
CHUME. Forgive us all.

> *And then, punctuated regularly with Amens . . .*

Yes, Father, make you forgive us all. Make you save us from palaver. Save us from trouble at home. Tell our wives not to give us trouble . . .

The PENITENT *has become placid. She is stretched out flat on the ground.*

... Tell our wives not to give us trouble. And give us money to have a happy home. Give us money to satisfy our daily necessities. Make you no forget those of us who dey struggle daily. Those who be clerk today, make them Chief Clerk tomorrow. Those who are Messenger today, make them Senior Service tomorrow. Yes Father, those who are Messenger today, make them Senior Service tomorrow.

The Amens grow more and more ecstatic.

Those who are petty trader today, make them big contractor tomorrow. Those who dey sweep street today, give them their own big office tomorrow. If we dey walka today, give us our own bicycle tomorrow. I say those who dey walka today, give them their own bicycle tomorrow. Those who have bicycle today, they will ride their own car tomorrow.

The enthusiasm of the response becomes, at this point quite overpowering.

I say those who dey push bicycle, give them big car tomorrow. Give them big car tomorrow. Give them big car tomorrow, give them big car tomorrow.

The angry WOMAN *comes again in view, striding with the same gait as before, but now in possession of the drums. A few yards behind, the* DRUMMER *jog-trots wretchedly, pleading.*

DRUMMER. I beg you, give me my drums. I take God's name beg you, I was not abusing your father ... For God's sake I beg you ... I was not abusing your father. I was only drumming ... I swear to God I was only drumming ...

They pass through.

PENITENT (*who has become much alive from the latter part of the prayers, pointing . . .*). Brother Jeroboam!

> BROTHER JERO *has just come in view. They all rush to help him back into the circle. He is a much altered man, his clothes torn and his face bleeding.*

JERO (*slowly and painfully*). Thank you, brother, sisters. Brother Chume, kindly tell these friends to leave me. I must pray for the soul of that sinful woman. I must say a personal prayer for her.

> CHUME *ushers them off. They go reluctantly, chattering excitedly.*

JERO. Prayers this evening, as usual. Late afternoon.

CHUME (*shouting after*). Prayers late afternoon as always. Brother Jeroboam says God keep you till then. Are you all right, Brother Jero?

JERO. Who would have thought that she would dare lift her hand against a prophet of God!

CHUME. Women are a plague, brother.

JERO. I had a premonition this morning that women would be my downfall today. But I thought of it only in the spiritual sense.

CHUME. Now you see how it is, Brother Jero.

JERO. From the moment I looked out of my window this morning I have been tormented one way or another by the Daughters of Discord.

CHUME (*eagerly*). That is how it is with me, Brother. Every day. Every morning and night. Only this morning she made me take her to the house of some poor man whom she says owes her money. She loaded enough on my bicycle to lay a siege for a week, and all the thanks I got was abuse.

JERO. Indeed, it must be a trial, Brother Chume ... and it requires great ...

He becomes suddenly suspicious.

Brother Chume, did you say that your wife went to make camp only this morning at the house of a ... of someone who owes her money?

CHUME. Yes, I took her there myself.

JERO. Er ... indeed, indeed. (*Coughs.*) Is ... your wife a trader?

CHUME. Yes, petty trading, you know. Wool, silk, cloth and all that stuff.

JERO. Indeed. Quite an enterprising woman. (*Hems.*) Er ... where was the house of this man ... I mean, this man who owes her money?

CHUME. Not very far from here. Ajete settlement, a mile or so from here. I did not even know the place existed until today.

JERO (*to himself*). So that is your wife ...

CHUME. Did you speak, Prophet?

JERO. No, no. I was only thinking how little women have changed since Eve, since Delilah, since Jezebel. But we must be strong of heart. I have my own cross too, Brother Chume. This morning alone I have been thrice in conflict with the daughters of discord. First there was ... no, never mind that. There is another who crosses my path every day. Goes to swim just over there and then waits for me to be in the midst of my meditation before she swings her hips across here, flaunting her near nakedness before my eyes ...

CHUME (*to himself with deep feeling*). I'd willingly change crosses with you.

JERO. What, Brother Chume?

CHUME. I was only praying.

JERO. Ah. That is the only way. But er ... I wonder really what the will of God would be in this matter. After all, Christ himself was not averse to using the whip when occasion demanded it.

CHUME (*eagerly*). No, he did not hesitate.

JERO. In that case, since, Brother Chume, your wife seems such a wicked, wilful sinner, I think . . .

CHUME. Yes, Holy One . . .?

JERO. You must take her home tonight . . .

CHUME. Yes . . .

JERO. And beat her.

CHUME (*kneeling, clasps* JERO's *hand in his*). Prophet!

JERO. Remember, it must be done in your own house. Never show the discord within your family to the world. Take her home and beat her.

> CHUME *leaps up and gets his bike.*

JERO. And Brother Chume . . .

CHUME. Yes, Prophet . . .

JERO. The Son of God appeared to me again this morning, robed just as he was when he named you my successor. And he placed his burning sword on my shoulder and called me his knight. He gave me a new title . . . but you must tell it to no one – yet.

CHUME. I swear, Brother Jero.

JERO (*staring into space*). He named me the Immaculate Jero, Articulate Hero of Christ's Crusade. (*Pauses, then, with a regal dismissal –*) You may go, Brother Chume.

CHUME. God keep you, Brother Jero – the Immaculate.

JERO. God keep you, brother. (*He sadly fingers the velvet cape.*)

> *Lights fade.*

SCENE FOUR

As Scene Two, i.e. in front of the prophet's home. Later that day.
CHUME *is just wiping off the last crumbs of yams on his plate.* AMOPE
watches him.

AMOPE. You can't say I don't try. Hounded out of house by
　debtors, I still manage to make you a meal.

CHUME (*sucking his fingers, sets down his plate*). It was a good
　meal, too.

AMOPE. I do my share as I've always done. I cooked you your
　meal. But when I ask you to bring me some clean water, you
　forget.

CHUME. I did not forget.

AMOPE. You keep saying that. Where is it then? Or perhaps the
　bottles fell off your bicycle on the way and got broken.

CHUME. That's a child's lie, Amope. You are talking to a man.

AMOPE. A fine man you are then, when you can't remember a
　simple thing like a bottle of clean water.

CHUME. I remembered. I just did not bring it. So that is that.
　And now pack up your things because we're going home.

　　AMOPE *stares at him unbelieving.*

CHUME. Pack up your things; you heard what I said.

AMOPE (*scrutinizing*). I thought you were a bit early to get back.
　You haven't been to work at all. You've been drinking all day.

CHUME. You may think what suits you. You know I never touch
　any liquor.

AMOPE. You needn't say it as if it was a virtue. You don't drink
　only because you cannot afford to. That is all the reason there is.

CHUME. Hurry. I have certain work to do when I get home and I
　don't want you delaying me.

AMOPE. Go then. I am not budging from here till I get my money.

> CHUME *leaps up, begins to throw her things into the bag.*
> BROTHER JERO *enters, hides and observes them.*

AMOPE (*quietly*). I hope you have ropes to tie me on the bicycle, because I don't intend to leave this place unless I am carried out. One pound eight shillings is no child's play. And it is my money, not yours.

> CHUME *has finished packing the bag and is now tying it on to the carrier.*

AMOPE. A messenger's pay isn't that much, you know – just in case you've forgotten you're not drawing a Minister's pay. So you better think again if you think I am letting my hard-earned money stay in the hands of that good-for-nothing. Just think, only this morning while I sat here, a Sanitary Inspector came along. He looked me all over and he made some notes in his book. Then he said, I suppose, woman, you realize that this place is marked down for slum clearance. This to me, as if I lived here. But you sit down and let your wife be exposed to such insults. And the Sanitary Inspector had a motor-cycle too, which is one better than a bicycle.

CHUME. You'd better be ready soon.

AMOPE. A Sanitary Inspector is a better job anyway. You can make something of yourself one way or another. They all do. A little here and a little there, call it bribery if you like, but see where *you've* got even though you don't drink or smoke or take bribes. He's got a motor-bike . . . anyway, who would want to offer kola to a Chief Messenger?

CHUME. Shut your big mouth!

AMOPE (*aghast*). What did you say?

CHUME. I said shut your big mouth.

AMOPE. To me?

CHUME. Shut your big mouth before I shut it for you. (*Ties the mat round the cross-bar.*) And you'd better start to watch your step from now on. My period of abstinence is over. My cross has been lifted off my shoulders by the prophet.

AMOPE (*genuinely distressed*). He's mad.

CHUME (*viciously tying up the mat*). My period of trial is over. (*Practically strangling the mat.*) If you so much as open your mouth now . . . (*Gives a further twist to the string.*)

AMOPE. God help me. He's gone mad.

CHUME (*imperiously*). Get on the bike.

AMOPE (*backing away*). I'm not coming with you.

CHUME. I said get on the bike!

AMOPE. Not with you. I'll find my own way home.

> CHUME *advances on her.* AMOPE *screams for help.* BROTHER JERO *crosses himself.* CHUME *catches her by the arm but she escapes, runs to the side of the house and beats on the door.*

AMOPE. Help! Open the door for God's sake. Let me in. Let me in . . .

> BROTHER JERO *grimaces.*

Is anyone in? Let me in for God's sake! Let me in or God will punish you!

JERO (*sticking his fingers in his ears*). Blasphemy!

AMOPE. Prophet! Where's the prophet?

> CHUME *lifts her bodily.*

AMOPE. Let me down! Police! Police!

CHUME (*setting her down*). If you shout just once more I'll . . . (*He raises a huge fist.*)

> BROTHER JERO *gasps in mock-horror, tut-tuts, covers his eyes with both hands and departs.*

AMOPE. Ho! You're mad. You're mad.

CHUME. Get on the bike.

AMOPE. Kill me! Kill me!

CHUME. Don't tempt me, woman!

AMOPE. I won't get on that thing unless you kill me first.

CHUME. Woman!

Two or three NEIGHBOURS *arrive, but keep a respectful distance.*

AMOPE. Kill me. You'll have to kill me. Everybody come and bear witness. He's going to kill me so come and bear witness. I forgive everyone who has ever done me evil. I forgive all my debtors especially the prophet who has got me into all this trouble. Prophet Jeroboam, I hope you will pray for my soul in heaven . . .

CHUME. You have no soul, wicked woman.

AMOPE. Brother Jeroboam, curse this man for me. You may keep the velvet cape if you curse this foolish man. I forgive you your debt. Go on, foolish man, kill me. If you don't kill me you won't do well in life.

CHUME (*suddenly*). Shut up!

AMOPE (*warming up as more people arrive*). Bear witness all of you. Tell the prophet I forgive him his debt but he must curse this foolish man to hell. Go on, kill me!

CHUME (*who has turned away, forehead knotted in confusion*). Can't you shut up, woman!

AMOPE. No, you must kill me . . .

The CROWD *hub bubs all the time, scared as always at the prospect of interfering in man-wife palaver, but throwing in half-hearted tokens of concern –*

'What's the matter, eh?' 'You too keep quiet.' 'Who are they?' 'Where is Brother Jero?' 'Do you think we ought to send for the

Prophet?' 'These women are so troublesome! Somebody go and
call Brother Jero.'

CHUME (*lifting* AMOPE's *head. She has, in the tradition of the 'Kill
me' woman, shut her eyes tightly and continued to beat her fists on
the prophet's door-step*). Shut up and listen. Did I hear you say
Prophet Jeroboam?

AMOPE. See him now. Let you bear witness. He's going to kill
me . . .

CHUME. I'm not touching you, but I will if you don't answer my
question.

AMOPE. Kill me . . . Kill me . . .

CHUME. Woman, did you say it was the prophet who owed you
money?

AMOPE. Kill me . . .

CHUME. Is this his house? (*Gives her head a shake.*) Does he live
here. . .?

AMOPE. Kill me . . . Kill me . . .

CHUME (*pushing her away in disgust and turning to the* CROWD.
They retreat instinctively). Is Brother Jeroboam . . .?

NEAREST ONE (*hastily*). No, no. I'm not Brother Jero. It's not
me.

CHUME. Who said you were? Does the prophet live here?

SAME MAN. Yes. Over there. That house.

CHUME (*turns round and stands stock still. Stares at the house for
quite some time*). So . . . so . . . so . . . so . . .

> *The* CROWD *is puzzled over his change of mood. Even* AMOPE
> *looks up wonderingly.* CHUME *walks towards his bicycle,
> muttering to himself.*

So . . . so . . . Suddenly he decides I may beat my wife, eh?
For his own convenience. At his own convenience.

> *He releases the bundle from the carrier, pushing it down care-
> lessly. He unties the mat also.*

BYSTANDER. What next is he doing now?

CHUME (*mounting his bicycle*). You stay here and don't move. If I don't find you here when I get back . . .

He rides off. They all stare at him in bewilderment.

AMOPE. He is quite mad. I have never seen him behave like that.

BYSTANDER. You are sure?

AMOPE. Am I sure? I'm his wife, so I ought to know, shouldn't I?

A WOMAN BYSTANDER. Then you ought to let the prophet see to him. I had a brother once who had the fits and foamed at the mouth every other week. But the prophet cured him. Drove the devils out of him, he did.

AMOPE. This one can't do anything. He's a debtor and that's all he knows. How to dodge his creditors.

She prepares to unpack her bundle.

Lights fade.

SCENE FIVE

The Beach. Nightfall.
A MAN *in an elaborate 'agbada' outfit, with long train and a cap is standing right, downstage, with a sheaf of notes in his hand. He is delivering a speech, but we don't hear it. It is undoubtedly a fire-breathing speech.*

The PROPHET JEROBOAM *stands bolt upright as always, surveying him with lofty compassion.*

JERO. I could teach him a trick or two about speech-making. He's a member of the Federal House, a back-bencher but with one eye on a ministerial post. Comes here every day to rehearse his speeches. But he never makes them. Too scared.

Pause. The PROPHET *continues to study the* MEMBER.

Poor fish. (*Chuckles and looks away.*) Oho, I had almost forgotten Brother Chume. By now he ought to have beaten his wife senseless. Pity! That means I've lost him. He is fulfilled and no longer needs me. True, he still has to become a Chief Clerk. But I have lost him as the one who was most dependent on me . . . Never mind, it was a good price to pay for getting rid of my creditor . . .

Goes back to the MEMBER.

Now he . . . he is already a member of my flock. He does not know it of course, but he is a follower. All I need do is claim him. Call him and say to him, My dear Member of the House, your place awaits you . . . Or do you doubt it? Watch me go to work on him. (*Raises his voice.*) My dear brother in Jesus!

The MEMBER *stops, looks round, resumes his speech.*

Dear brother, do I not know you?

MEMBER *stops, looks round again.*

Yes, you. In God's name, do I not know you?

MEMBER *approaches slowly.*

Yes indeed. It is you. And you come as it was predicted. Do you not perhaps remember me?

MEMBER *looks at him scornfully.*

Then you cannot be of the Lord. In another world, in another body, we met, and my message was for you . . .

The MEMBER *turns his back impatiently.*

MEMBER (*with great pomposity*). Go and practise your fraudulences on another person of greater gullibility.

JERO (*very kindly, smiling*). Indeed the matter is quite plain. You are not of the Lord. And yet such is the mystery of God's ways that his favour has lighted upon you . . . Minister . . . Minister by the grace of God . . .

The MEMBER *stops dead.*

Yes, brother, we have met. I saw this country plunged into strife. I saw the mustering of men, gathered in the name of peace through strength. And at a desk, in a large gilt room, great men of the land awaited your decision. Emissaries of foreign nations hung on your word, and on the door leading into your office, I read the words, Minister for War . . .

The MEMBER *turns round slowly.*

. . . It is a position of power. But are you of the Lord? Are you in fact worthy? Must I, when I have looked into your soul, as the Lord has commanded me to do, must I pray to the Lord to remove this mantle from your shoulders and place it on a more God-fearing man?

The MEMBER *moves forward unconsciously. The* PROPHET *gestures him to stay where he is. Slowly –*

Yes . . . I think I see Satan in your eyes. I see him entrenched in your eyes . . .

The MEMBER *grows fearful, raises his arms in half-supplication.*

The Minister for War would be the most powerful position in the Land. The Lord knows best, but he has empowered his lieutenants on earth to intercede where necessary. We can reach him by fasting and by prayer ... we can make recommendations ... Brother, are you of God or are you ranged among his enemies ...?

JEROBOAM's *voice fades away and the light also dims on him as another voice –* CHUME's *– is heard long before he is seen.* CHUME *enters from left, downstage, agitated and talking to himself.*

CHUME. ... What for ... why, why, why, why 'e do 'am? For two years 'e no let me beat that woman. Why? No because God no like 'am. That one no fool me any more. 'E no be man of God. 'E say 'in sleep for beach whether 'e rain or cold but that one too na big lie. The man get house and 'e sleep there every night. But 'in get peace for 'in house, why 'e no let me get peace for mine? Wetin I do for 'am? Anyway, how they come meet? Where? When? What time 'e know say na my wife? Why 'e dey protect 'am from me? Perhaps na my woman dey give 'am chop and in return he promise to see say 'in husband no beat 'am. A-a-a-ah, give 'am clothes, give 'am food and all comforts and necessities, and for exchange, 'in go see that 'in husband no beat 'am ... Mmmmmm.

He shakes his head.

No, is not possible. I no believe that. If na so, how they come quarrel then. Why she go sit for front of 'in house demand all 'in money. I no beat 'am yet ...

He stops suddenly. His eyes slowly distend.

Almighty! Chume, fool! O God, my life done spoil. My life done spoil finish. O God a no' get eyes for my head. Na lie. Na big lie. Na pretence 'e de pretend that wicked woman! She no' go collect nutin! She no' mean to sleep for outside house. The Prophet na 'in lover. As soon as 'e dark, she go in go meet 'in man. O God, wetin a do for you wey you go spoil my life so? Wetin make you vex for me so? I offend you? Chume, foolish man, your life done spoil. Your life done spoil. Yeah, ye . . . ah ah, ye-e-ah, they done ruin Chume for life . . . ye-e-ah, ye-e-ah . . .

He goes off, his cries dying off-stage.
Light up slowly on JERO. *The* MEMBER *is seen kneeling now at* BROTHER JERO's *feet, hands clasped and shut eyes raised to heaven. . .*

JERO (*his voice gaining volume*). Protect him therefore. Protect him when he must lead this country as his great ancestors have done. He comes from the great warriors of the land. In his innocence he was not aware of this heritage. But you know everything and you plan it all. There is no end, no beginning . . .

CHUME *rushes in, brandishing a cutlass.*

CHUME. Adulterer! Woman-thief! Na today a go finish you!

JERO *looks round.*

JERO. God save us! (*Flees.*)
MEMBER (*unaware of what is happening*). Amen.

CHUME *follows out* JERO, *murder-bent.*

MEMBER. Amen. Amen. (*Opens his eyes.*) Thank you, proph . . .

He looks right, left, back, front, but he finds the PROPHET *has really disappeared.*

Prophet! Prophet! (*Turns sharply and rapidly in every direction, shouting.*) Prophet, where are you? Where have you gone? Prophet! Don't leave me, Prophet, don't leave me!

He looks up slowly, with awe.

Vanished. Transported. Utterly transmuted. I knew it. I knew I stood in the presence of God . . .

He bows his head, standing. JEROBOAM *enters quite collected, and points to the convert.*

JERO. You heard him. With your own ears you heard him. By tomorrow, the whole town will have heard about the miraculous disappearance of Brother Jeroboam. Testified to and witnessed by no less a person than one of the elected rulers of the country . . .

MEMBER (*goes to sit on the mound*). I must await his return. If I show faith, he will show himself again to me . . . (*Leaps up as he is about to sit.*) This is holy ground. (*Takes off his shoes and sits.*) I must hear further from him. Perhaps he has gone to learn more about this ministerial post . . . (*Sits.*)

JERO. I have already sent for the police. It is a pity about Chume. But he has given me a fright, and no prophet likes to be frightened. With the influence of that nincompoop I should succeed in getting him certified with ease. A year in the lunatic asylum would do him good anyway.

The MEMBER *is already nodding.*

Good . . . He is falling asleep. When I appear again to him he'll think I have just fallen from the sky. Then I'll tell him that

Satan just sent one of his emissaries into the world under the name of Chume, and that he had better put him in a strait-jacket at once . . . And so the day is saved. The police will call on me here as soon as they catch Chume. And it looks as if it is not quite time for the fulfilment of that spiteful man's prophecy.

He picks up a pebble and throws it at the MEMBER. *At the same time a ring of red or some equally startling colour plays on his head, forming a sort of halo. The* MEMBER *wakes with a start, stares open-mouthed, and falls flat on his face, whispering in rapt awe –*

MEMBER. 'Master!'

Blackout.

THE END

JERO'S METAMORPHOSIS

CAST

BROTHER JEROBOAM

SISTER REBECCA

ANANAIAS

CHIEF EXECUTIVE OFFICER

CLERK TO THE TOURIST BOARD

CHUME

MAJOR SILVA

SHADRACH ⎫

CALEB ⎬ *and other Beach Prophets*

ISAAC ⎪

MATTHEW ⎭

A POLICEWOMAN

SCENE ONE

BROTHER JERO's *office. It is no longer his rent-troubled shack of* The Trials *but a modest white-washed room, quite comfortable. A 'surplus-store' steel cabinet is tucked in a corner. On a cloth-covered table is an ancient beat-up typewriter of the oldest imaginable model but functioning. A vase of flowers, the usual assortment of professional paraphernalia – bible, prayer-book, chasuble, etc. etc.*
On the wall, a large framed picture of a uniformed figure at a battery of microphones indicates that JERO's *diocese is no longer governed by his old friends the civilian politicians. As* JERO *dictates, striding up and down the room, it is obvious that he has his mind very much on this photograph. A demure young woman, quite attractive, is seated at a table taking the dictation.*

JERO. . . . in time of trouble it behoves us to come together, to forget old enmities and bury the hatchet in the head of a common enemy . . . no, better take that out. It sounds a little unchristian wouldn't you say?

REBECCA (*her voice and manner are of unqualified admiration*). Not if you don't think it, Brother Jeroboam.

JERO. Well, we have to be careful about our brother prophets. Some of them might just take it literally. The mere appearance of the majority of them, not to mention their secret past and even secret present . . . ah well, stop at 'bury the hatchet'.

REBECCA. Whatever you say, Brother Jeroboam.

JERO. Not that I would regret it. We could do with the elevation to eternity of some of our dearly beloved brother prophets on this beach, and if they choose the way of the hangman's noose or elect to take the latest short cut to heaven facing a firing squad at the Bar Beach Show,* who are we to dispute such a divine solution? Only trouble is, it might give the rest of us a bad name.

REBECCA. Nothing could give you a bad name, Brother Jero. You stand apart from the others. Nothing can tarnish your image, I know that.

JERO. You are indeed kind, Sister Rebecca. I don't know what I would do without you.

REBECCA. You won't ever have to do without me, Brother Jero. As long as you need me, I'll be here.

JERO. Hm, yes, hm. (*The prospect makes him nervous.*) I thank you, Sister. Now we must get back to work. Read me the last thing I dictated.

REBECCA. . . . in time of trouble it behoves us to get together, to forget old enemies and bury the hatchet in the head . . . no, we stop at 'hatchet'.

JERO. Good. I have therefore decided to summon – no, invite is better wouldn't you say? The more miserable they are the more touchy and proud you'll find them. The monster of pride feeds upon vermin, Sister Rebecca. The hole in a poor man's garment is soon filled with the patchwork of pride, so resolutely does Nature abhor a vacuum.

REBECCA. Oh Brother Jero, you say such wise things.

JERO. I have but little gifts, Sister Rebecca, but I make the most of them. Yes, let the phrase read – after much prayer for guidance, I am inspired to invite you all to a meeting where we shall all, as equals before God and servants of his will, deliberate and find a way to stop this threat to our vocation. In our own mutual interest – underline that heavily – in our own mutual interest, I trust that all shepherds of the Lord whose pastures are upon this sandy though arable beach will make it their duty to be present.

---

* Popular expression for the new fashion of public executions in Lagos, capital of Nigeria.

He shakes his head as if to clear it, goes to a small cupboard and brings out a bottle. Pouring a drink.

The gall is bitter, Sister Rebecca. The burden is heavy upon me.

REBECCA. It has to be done, Brother Jero. The end will justify the means.

JERO. To fraternize with those cut-throats, dope-pedlars, smugglers and stolen goods receivers? Some of them are ex-convicts do you know that? Some of them are long overdue for the Bar Beach Spectacular.

REBECCA. The more noble of you in sinking your pride and meeting with them in the service of God.

JERO (*offering a glass*). You will join me, Sister Rebecca?

REBECCA. No, Brother Jero, but you must have one.

JERO. You are sure it is not wrong?

REBECCA. All things are God's gifts. It is not wrong to use them wisely.

JERO. You comfort me greatly, Sister Rebecca. The times are indeed trying. Believe me, it is no time for half-measures.

REBECCA. Brother Jero, you promised . . .

JERO. Oh I didn't mean this half-measure. (*Tosses down drink.*)

REBECCA. Forgive me, I . . .

JERO. A natural error. No, I was referring to our present predicament. To survive, we need full-bodied tactics.

REBECCA. I know you will find a way.

JERO. It seems to me that in our upward look to heaven for a solution we have neglected what inspiration is afforded us below. Yes, indeed we have.

REBECCA. Has earth anything to offer the true Christian, Brother Jero? How often have you said yourself . . .

JERO. That was before I read this precious file which you brought to Christ as your dowry. An unparalleled dowry in the history of spiritual marriages Sister Rebecca. And before . . . (*He takes down the picture on the wall, inspects it at arm's length nodding with satisfaction.*) . . . yes, I think we have neglected our earthly inspirations.

REBECCA. But Brother Jero . . .

JERO. Trust me, Sister Rebecca.

REBECCA. I do, Brother Jero, I do.

JERO. The voice of the people is the voice of God, did you know that Sister?

REBECCA. I trust you. I follow wherever you lead me, Brother Jeroboam.

JERO. I shall lead you to safety, you and all who put their faith in me.

REBECCA. Instruct me, Brother Jero.

JERO (*hanging up the picture*). Distribute those invitations at once. Go to my tailor and ask him to deliver my order tonight. Prepare everything for the spiritual assembly. When the moment comes, all shall be made plain.

REBECCA. I am with you to the end.

JERO. When the tailor delivers the order, you will understand.

REBECCA (*looking at the notes*). You did not fix a time for the meeting.

JERO. Tonight, Sister, at eight. We have no time to lose.

> *He picks up his chasuble, drapes it round his neck, his holy rod, bible etc. Then he picks up the file again, opens it at a page and smiles, nodding with satisfaction, pats the file tenderly.*

Our secret weapon, Sister Rebecca. We must take good care of it.

> *Locks it up in a cabinet.*

REBECCA. You are going out Brother Jero?

JERO. Preparations, Sister, preparations. If we must fight this battle well, there is a certain ally we cannot do without. I must go and seek him.

He stops. Benevolent smile.

But we shall win, Sister Rebecca, we shall win. Because I have already the best ally on my side. Here, in this room.

Going, hesitates, moves towards the vase of flowers and raises it to his face, sniffing delicately with his eyes shut.

And I thank you for brightening up my humble shack with these flowers, even as you have lightened my life with your spiritual lamp.

Goes out rapidly, leaving SISTER REBECCA *coy, enraptured, confused and overwhelmed all at once.*
Once outdoors BROTHER JERO *slips round the side and observes her through a window. The woman's condition obviously uplifts him for he moves off with even jauntier step and a light adjustment to his chasuble. He is immediately confronted by a fellow prophet,* ANANAIAS, *one of the poorer specimens of the brotherhood but built like a barrel.*

ANANAIAS. What are you up to now, Jero? Spying on your own little nest?

JERO (*clamps his hand on* ANANAIAS *and drags him off*). S-sh.

ANANAIAS. Take your hands off me. (*Shakes him off easily but follows him.*) So who have you got in there? The bailiffs?

JERO. Bailiffs like all sinners are welcome in my church, Brother Ananaias. But I do not welcome them in my humble abode.

ANANAIAS. That's enough of that pious nonsense. I know you.

JERO. Just what do you know of me, Brother?

ANANAIAS. Eh, come off it. If it's bailiffs . . .

JERO. Bailiffs do not even know my dwelling Ananaias.

ANANAIAS. That's because you're a clever man, Jero. Not even your worst enemy will deny you that.

JERO. Will you kindly say what business brought you here? I'm a busy man.

ANANAIAS. All right, then. I came to tell you you're going to need all that cunning of yours very soon. The City Council have taken a final decision. They're going to chuck us out. Every last hypocritical son of the devil.

JERO. That is old news, Ananaias. And for some of us it doesn't matter of course. The Lord will provide. But for those with no true vocation . . .

ANANAIAS. Like you.

JERO. I said vocation. You wouldn't know what that is. The beach for you is just a living, nothing else.

ANANAIAS. You haven't done badly out of it yourself I notice.

JERO. It is written that the good Lord shall feed his true servants. What are you going to do when you wake up one morning and find yourself face to face with a bulldozer?

ANANAIAS (*flexing his muscles*). Let them try that's all, let them try.

JERO. Wrestling is one thing but a bulldozer is another. Not even you can wrestle a bulldozer. And let me tell you, you are getting no younger.

ANANAIAS. Am I a born fool? There's a man drives those clumsy beasts isn't there? I leave the machine alone and drag him out by the scruff of his neck. When I've dipped him in the sea a few times he will emerge a good Christian and learn how to leave holy prophets alone.

JERO. That's not the way to fight them.

ANANAIAS. What's the way then? Stand by? Let them run me out of this land of milk and honey? I was doing quite well as a wrestler before I got the call and came into the service of the Lord. Gave all that up for this barren waste and now I can't even call it my own?

JERO. A moment ago it was a land of milk and honey.

ANANAIAS. Spiritual milk and honey of course. Otherwise barren waste. Look at it yourself.

JERO. Violence will not help us. I am calling a meeting tonight at

which all these matters will be discussed. The good Lord shall
help us find a way.

ANANAIAS. Calling a meeting? You already have something up
your sleeve or you wouldn't be calling a meeting. Come on, let's
have it. Let's be partners, you and me.

JERO. Tonight.

ANANAIAS. Now. Or I'll go in that room and tell whoever is
there you were hiding and spying on them. I'll shout and tell
them you're right here.

JERO (*folding his arms*). Go ahead, then.

ANANAIAS. Hey?

JERO. I said go ahead.

ANANAIAS. You're bluffing you know.

JERO. Call my bluff then. And by the way, when the battle is over
and we have won our rights, I shall run you off this beach
without lifting a finger.

ANANAIAS. You can't do that to me. I've got as much right as you
to be here.

JERO. Not you.

ANANAIAS. You can't do it. I'm a holy man same as you.

JERO (*contemptuously*). Wrestling. Were you also wrestling in
Kiri-kiri Prisons?

ANANAIAS (*clamping his hand over JERO's mouth in turn, and
staring wildly round*). You're the devil himself you are. How
come you know that?

JERO. I know.

ANANAIAS (*suddenly*). What of it? So I did a bit of thieving before
and got nabbed. But I've been straight ever since. Earned my
living wrestling for pick-ups clean and honest. And then I got
the call. I'm reformed. What's wrong with a reformed sinner?

JERO. Reformed sinner? Hm. You didn't by any chance thug for
a certain businessman just this last week did you? A little trade
war over the monopoly of the whisky retail trade. Whisky
Ananaias, whisky!

ANANAIAS (*dignified*). I beg your pardon, Brother Jero. I never was no thug in all my life. Bodyguard, yes. Bodyguard I was, and whoever says that is not a respectable position, internationally recognized, I'd just like to meet him that's all.

JERO. The police still have the fingerprints of the man who set fire to the store of one of the trade rivals. Bottles of spirits exploding all night and injuring innocent people. And the dumb, gross, incompetent all-muscle-and-no-brain petty criminal left a hefty thumbprint on the kerosene tin and then threw the kerosene tin on a refuse heap near by. They also know that that dirty great print matches the thumbprint of a certain ex-convict. The only thing they don't know is where he is hiding out after crimes of arson, unlawful wounding, attempted murder . . .

ANANAIAS (*swallowing hard*). Brother Jero . . .

JERO. Even the tin of kerosene was stolen from a near-by shop . . . that was robbery. Did you also use violence, Ananaias?

ANANAIAS. I swear to God, Brother Jero . . .

JERO. You are known to be a violent man. The Prosecutor can make it robbery with violence. And you know what that means.

ANANAIAS. I mean to say, Brother Jero, you are pretty hard on a man. You know yourself business is slow . . . A man must eat . . .

JERO *lets him squirm a little.*

JERO. Tonight at the meeting I shall put forward certain plans . . .

ANANAIAS. I'll support you, Brother, depend on my vote any time. (*Getting warmer.*) And if there's anyone you'd prefer to take a walk outside on his head for making trouble . . .

JERO. I don't need your violence thank you. (*Going.*) And keep away from this place until meeting time.

ANANAIAS (*running after him*). I say Brother, Brother . . .

JERO. Well?

ANANAIAS. Brother Jero. Could you lend me a shilling or two till the meeting? You know I wouldn't ask if . . . you . . . well you see how it is yourself. Things haven't been going well lately. No contribution, nothing at all. The congregation have shrunk to nothing and even them as comes, all I get is the story of their family troubles. They no longer pay tithes.

JERO. You were greedy, Brother Ananaias. If every man of a hundred congregation paid a tithe at the end of every month he is going to notice very soon that a tithe from everyone means several times what each man is earning. And all that for one man – you – alone! That's why they stopped coming.

ANANAIAS. Heh?

JERO. Yes, that's how you lost your little flock.

ANANAIAS. From a hundred to nothing!

JERO. From a hundred to nothing, except those who come to borrow money.

ANANAIAS. But how come such an idea enter their head? I would never have thought of it.

JERO (*handing him a shilling*). Perhaps *somebody* put it in their head. Good day, Ananaias.

ANANAIAS. Heh? (*Stands open-mouthed, gaping at the retreating* JERO.)

From the opposite side, the CHIEF EXECUTIVE OFFICER *of the Tourist Board of the City Council emerges, rumpled and dusty from his hiding place. He is followed by the* CLERK *to the Board and a* POLICEWOMAN. ANANAIAS *hides and observes.*

CLERK. This is the place, sir.

EXECUTIVE (*angrily brushing his bowler hat and suit. The* CLERK *helps him*). About time too. I shall deal very rigorously with all of you who subjected me to this most humiliating adventure. Come all this way to lose not only a confidential file but a Confidential Secretary. Why I should be the one to be saddled with their recovery . . .

CLERK. Sir, it is the only way . . .

EXECUTIVE. Nothing unbecoming to a man's dignity is ever the only way. Bear that in mind.

CLERK. To achieve results sir . . .

EXECUTIVE. Kindly stop arguing with me. It is not in my character to skulk and hide until a mere charlatan is out of the way. I prefer to confront him squarely even if he's the devil himself.

CLERK. Sir, please let's enter and get the business over. He may return any time.

EXECUTIVE. If you are planning for me to escape through the window if he returns suddenly . . .

CLERK. Nothing of the sort, sir, nothing of the sort. I only say time is money, sir. Let's go in.

> *He knocks on the door but the* CHIEF EXECUTIVE *barges in.* REBECCA *looks startled at their entrance.* ANANAIAS *creeps closer. The* POLICEWOMAN *waits by the door.*

EXECUTIVE. Is this the woman?

CLERK. Yes, sir. Miss Denton, this is the Chief Executive Officer of the Tourist Board of the City Council. Miss Denton, sir.

EXECUTIVE. Miss Denton . . .

REBECCA. My name is Rebecca.

EXECUTIVE. I do not believe, young lady, that we are on Christian name terms.

REBECCA. I do not believe that you are on Christian terms at all, sir. Your soul is in danger.

EXECUTIVE (*splutters badly and explodes*). My religious state is no concern of yours, young woman.

REBECCA. But it is, sir, it is. I am my brother's keeper. The state of your soul distresses me, sir.

CLERK. That's how it started, sir. That's how it started.

EXECUTIVE. That is how what started?

CLERK. That was how the prophet got her. He wasn't even addressing her at all but the C.E.O. who came to serve him notice. He kept preaching at him all the time but she was the one who got the message. Christ sir, you should have seen her convulsions!

EXECUTIVE. Why the hell did he bring her in the first place?

REBECCA. Hell is true sir. I was living in hell but did not know it until Brother Jero pointed the path of God to me.

EXECUTIVE. I was not addressing you, woman.

CLERK. She was his private secretary . . .

EXECUTIVE. I know she was his private secretary, damn you . . .

REBECCA. He will not be damned sir, the Lord is merciful . . .

EXECUTIVE. Can't anyone shut up this religious maniac? I asked, why bring her along? Do you see me here with my private secretary?

REBECCA. I shall answer that question. When you are saved, you are no longer afraid to tell the truth. My boss asked me to come with him to take notes, but in my heart I knew that he was planning to seduce me.

EXECUTIVE. What! You dare slander a senior government official of my department in my presence? I shall order an investigation and have you charged with . . .

CLERK. Don't, sir. It's the truth. The C.E.O. has had his eye on her a long time. Wouldn't let her alone in the office, making her do overtime even if there was no work to do, just to try and . . .

EXECUTIVE. That's enough thank you. I don't need the whole picture painted in bold and dirty colours.

CLERK. Yes, sir, I mean, no, sir.

REBECCA. Do not distress yourself for that poor sinner. I pray for the salvation of his soul every day.

EXECUTIVE. And we are praying for you to come to your senses. And for a start just hand me the file you had with you. And be thankful I am not having you charged for keeping an official file after office hours.

CLERK. And a confidential file don't forget that, sir. Very confidential.

EXECUTIVE. Quite right. The file, young lady. We will overlook the offence since you weren't really in possession of your senses.

REBECCA. I was never more clearly within my senses as now.

EXECUTIVE. You call this a sensible action? You, an intelligent young girl, a fully trained Confidential Secretary . . .

CLERK. Eighty words per minute, sir, one hundred and twenty shorthand . . .

EXECUTIVE. Did I ask you to supply me statistics?

CLERK. Beg pardon, sir. Just saying what a waste it is.

EXECUTIVE. Of course it's a bloody waste. Eighty words per minute and a hundred and twenty shorthand. You had enough will-power to resist the revolting advances of a lecherous Chief Eviction Officer on the rampage, you are trusted sufficiently to be assigned an official duty which is most essential to our national economy and what happens – you permit yourself to be bamboozled by a fake prophet, a transparent charlatan . . .

REBECCA (*pitying*). It is the devil which speaks in you sir, it's the devil which makes you call Prophet Jeroboam all those bad names.

EXECUTIVE. He deserves more than a bad name. He deserves a bad end and he will come to it yet.

REBECCA. Fight the devil in you, sir, let us help you fight and conquer him.

EXECUTIVE. Can't you see Jeroboam is the devil, damn you? All the prophets on this beach are devils . . .

REBECCA. The devil is in you, sir, I can see him.

EXECUTIVE. They have to be evicted. They stand in the way of progress. They clutter up the beach and prevent decent men from coming here and paying to enjoy themselves. They are holding up a big tourist business. You know yourself how the land value has doubled since we started public executions on this beach.

REBECCA. Shameless sinners who acquire wealth from the misfortunes of others? Will you make money off sin and iniquity? Oh sir, you must let Brother Jero talk to you about the evil in your plans. To make money out of sin is to bring sin upon the dwellers of your city. Not Sodom nor Gomorrah shall suffer as this city of yours when the wrath of the Lord descends upon it and the walls are wiped off the surface of the earth. The Lord speaks in me. I am the mouthpiece of his will. Give up this plan and let the prophets continue the blessed task of turning men back to the path of goodness and decency . . .

EXECUTIVE. Shut her up. For God's sake shut her up.

REBECCA (*sudden joy*). Praise the Lord! A change has begun in you already. When you first came in you called on hell and you damned your fellow man. Now you call out in God's name. Hallelujah! Hallelujah! Hallelujah! Come to me, said the Lord. Call my name and I shall answer. Hallelujah! Hallelujah! Call his name and he shall heed you. Come to me, said the Lord, come to me. Come to me, said the Lord, come to me. Come to me, said the Lord, come to me. Call my name, and I shall heed you. Turn from sin and I shall feed you. Turn from filth and I shall cleanse you. Turn from filth and I shall cleanse you.

She approaches the EXECUTIVE OFFICER *with outstretched arms as if to embrace him. He retreats round the room but she follows him. She gets progressively 'inspired'.*

Give up the plan, said the Lord, give up the plan. What avails all the wealth of the world, if your soul is lost. What avails your cars and houses if you'll burn in hell. Save this sinner, Lord save his soul. Burn out the greed of his heart, burn out the greed.

The CHIEF EXECUTIVE *makes the door but* ANANAIAS, *with a roar of 'Hallelujah' steps out and blocks it. The* CHIEF EXECUTIVE *flings himself back into the room, bang into the arms of* REBECCA *who with a shout of 'Hallelujah' holds him in an unbreakable embrace. His bowler hat is knocked off and he soon parts company with his umbrella. The* CLERK *retreats to the corner of the room on seeing* ANANAIAS, *while the* POLICE-WOMAN *who tries to squeeze past* ANANAIAS *is herself swept up with one arm and held there by* ANANAIAS.

ANANAIAS. And this sinner, lord, and this sinner!

REBECCA. Hallelujah!

ANANAIAS. From her labour of sin, oh Lord, from her labour of sin.

REBECCA. Hallelujah!

ANANAIAS. Policework is evil, oh lord, policework is evil.

REBECCA. Halle-Halle-Hallelujah. (*And continues the chorus.*)

ANANAIAS. Save this sinner, Lord, save this sinner. Protect her from bribery, oh Lord! Protect her from corruption! Protect her from iniquities known and unknown, from practices unmentionable in thy hearing. Protect her from greed for promotion, from hunger for stripes, from chasing after citations with actions over and beyond the call of duty. Save her from harassing the innocent and molesting the tempted, from prying into the affairs of men and nosing out their innocent practices. Take out the beam in thine own eye, said the Lord.

REBECCA. Hallelujah!

ANANAIAS. Take out the beam in thine own eye!

REBECCA. Hallelujah!

ANANAIAS. Take out the beam in thine own eye, for who shall cast the first stone sayeth the Lord! Let him that hath no sin cast the first stone! Let him that hath no sin make the first arrest! Vengeance is mine saith the Lord, I shall recompense. Vengeance is mine, take not the law into your own hands! Verily I say unto you it is easier for a camel to pass through a needle's eye than for a police man or woman to enter the kingdom of heaven. We pray you bring them into the kingdom of heaven Lord. Bring them into the kingdom of heaven Lord. Bring them into the kingdom of heaven Lord. Bring them all into the kingdom of heaven. Save them from this hatred of their fellow men, from this hatred of poor weak vessels who merely seek a modest living. Oh bring them into the kingdom of heaven Lord. Right up to the kingdom of heaven Lord. Right into the kingdom of heaven. . .

REBECCA's *ecstasy has reached such proportions that she is*

trembling from head to foot. Suddenly she flings out her arms,
knocking off the glasses of the EXECUTIVE OFFICER.

REBECCA. Into the kingdom of heaven Lord, into the kingdom of
heaven. . .

EXECUTIVE OFFICER *seizes his freedom on the instant, dives*
through the window headfirst. The CLERK *is about to help him*
pick up his fallen bowler and umbrella but changes his mind as
ANANAIAS *steps forward. He follows his master through the*
window. ANANAIAS *in making for the fallen trophy lets go the*
POLICEWOMAN *who makes for safety through the door.*
REBECCA *is completely oblivious to all the goings-on, only*
gyrating and repeating 'into the kingdom of heaven . . .'
ANANAIAS *picks up the umbrella and bowler, looks in the*
cupboard and pockets a piece of bread he finds there, sniffs the
bottle and downs the contents. Finding nothing else that can be
lifted, he shrugs and starts to leave. Stops, takes another look at
the yet ecstatic REBECCA, *goes over to a corner of the room and*
lifts up a bucket of water, throws it on SISTER REBECCA. *She*
is stopped cold and shudders. Exit ANANAIAS, *taking the*
bucket with him.

SCENE TWO

A portrait of the uniformed figure, in a different pose, hangs over the
veranda of the house where CHUME *lives in rented rooms. He is*
practising on a trumpet, trying out the notes of 'What a friend we
have in Jesus'. His Salvation Army uniform is laid out carefully on
a chair, stiffly starched and newly ironed. Enter MAJOR SILVA, *also*
of the Salvation Army.

SILVA (*his accent is perfect RP plus a blend of Oxford*). Good day, Corporal Chummy. I'm afraid the Captain could not come today, but I will do my humble best to deputize for him. (*Points to the trumpet and the sheet music.*) I am glad to notice that you at least do some homework.

CHUME *looks at him with a mixture of suspicion and hostility.*

CHUME. How can? You don't yourself blow trumpet.

SILVA. That indeed is true, but I do understand music and that really is what I intend to teach. Well, shall we begin?

CHUME. Where is Captain Winston?

SILVA. I have told you, he is unable to come. Now, if you will just tell me how far you have progressed with him we shall er, see what we can do eh?

CHUME (*obviously dissatisfied*). It is much better for man to have only one teacher. I begin get used to Captain Winston and then somebody else comes. Captain Winston understand how to teach me.

SILVA. Well, if you gave me a chance, Chummy, I think I may be able to fill Captain Winston's shoes for a lesson at least, with God's help. Well now . . .

CHUME. I think . . . well, we can wait. I mean I can just practise by myself until . . .

SILVA. Now now, Chummy, we haven't got all day you know. Here, let's start with this shall we? Let's hear you play this piece, enh. (*Selecting a sheet from the pile.*) Then I can form some sort of idea. Right? Just play it once through.

CHUME. No, I don't want to play that one.

SILVA. Oh? All right. What do you wish to play? Pick out another one . . . anything you like. What hymn did you last practise with the Captain?

CHUME. I don't know. We just dey practise that's all.

SILVA. Well, play me what you last practised then.

CHUME. We practise hymn upon hymn. Er – one hymn like that, but I don't remember the name.

SILVA. Well, give me the first few bars and we will go from there. Right?

CHUME, obviously still uncomfortable, lifts the trumpet to his lips.

Good. After four. One – Two – Three – Four.

CHUME sets upon 'What a friend we have in Jesus', SILVA listens, registers mild surprise and shrugs. He waits for CHUME to finish a verse.

But that is the music I picked for you. I thought you said you didn't want to play it.

CHUME. En-hen? I change my mind.

SILVA. All right. Now, Chummy, this time try and play what is written down here. Stick it on your trumpet please. You see, you cannot give church hymns your own rhythm. You have to play what has been put down, so please read the score and play.

CHUME. I no talk so? I say is better to wait for Captain Winston. You can't understand how to teach me properly.

SILVA. Now, now, let's stop all this silliness. Here, let's have another go. It's all a matter of tempo, Chummy, tempo – Tam. ta. ra. ta. ra. ta. tam . . . tam . . . tam . . . ta. ra. ta. ra. ta. tam . . . Sharp and precise, Chummy, not like high life or juju music. Now shall we try again? This time, follow the score.

He hands the sheet to CHUME who sticks it on his trumpet.

Now, are we ready? One – Two – Three . . . Tam . . . ta. ra . . .

CHUME plays the tune in the same swingy beat and SILVA stops him.

SILVA. No, no, tempo, Chummy, tempo ... good God! (*Coming round to point out the score.*) Corporal, do you always read music upside down?

CHUME. Hm? (*Guiltily begins to re-set the card,* SILVA *looks at him with increasing suspicion.*) No wonder ... en-hen, that's better.

SILVA (*severely.*) Corporal Chummy, can you read music notation at all?

CHUME (*angrily*). I no talk so? You done come with your trouble. I say I go wait for Captain Winston you say you go fit teach me. Now you come dey bother me with music notation. Na paper man dey take trumpet play abi na music?

SILVA. Can you read music or not, Brother Chummy?

CHUME. Can you play trumpet or not, Major Silva?

SILVA. Really this is too much. How can Captain Winston expect me to teach you anything when you are musically illiterate.

CHUME. So I am illiterate now? I am illiterate? You are illiterate yourself. Illiterate man yourself.

SILVA. What! All right let us keep our temper.

CHUME. I have not lost my temper, it is you who don't know where you leave your own. You no even sabbe call my name correct and you dey call man illiterate. My name na Chume, no to Chummy.

SILVA (*with superhuman effort*). Anger, the Christian soldier's anger must be reserved only for the enemies of God and righteousness. It has no place within the army of God itself. Please bow your head, Corporal Chummy. I beg your pardon – Choo-may.

> *He strikes an attitude of prayer and* CHUME *obediently does likewise. They remain silent for several moments.*

May God give us strength against the sin of false pride and the devil of wrath, Amen.

CHUME. Amen.

SILVA. And now we shall begin all over again. (*Taking off the music card.*) We will forget all about this for the moment shall we? Captain Winston said that you were a natural on the trumpet and I suppose he is right. But there are certain things still to be learnt otherwise you will be like a lone voice crying in the wilderness. Now, shall we try again? I want you to watch me and try and follow the er, the movement of my hands – like this. Watch, watch . . . Tam . . . ta. ra. ta. tam. ta. ra . . . tam and so on. Got it?

CHUME (*assertively*). Yes, yes. That is how Captain Winston is teaching me.

SILVA. Good. Now are we ready? One – Two – Three . . .

Continues to talk as he plays.

That's better. Always remember that the tunes of the Army must be martial in colour and tempo. We march to it remember, not dance. No, no. Stop. No flourishes please, no flourishes. Especially not with a march. Most especially not with a march.

CHUME. Which one be flourish again?

SILVA. Beg your pardon?

CHUME. I say which one be flourish?

SILVA. Oh, flourish. Well, flourish is er . . . extra, you know, frills, decoration. What we want is pure notes, pure crystal clear notes. (CHUME *looks blank.*) Look, just play the first bar again will you.

CHUME (*more mystified still*). Bar?

SILVA. Yes, the first . . . all right, start from the beginning again will you and I will stop you when you come to the flourish . . .

CHUME *plays.* SILVA *stops him after a few notes.*

That's it. You played that bit Ta-a-ta instead of ta-ta.

CHUME. Oh you mean the pepper.

SILVA. Pepper?

CHUME. Enh, pepper. When you cook soup you go put small pepper. Otherwise the thing no go taste. I mean to say, 'e go taste like something, After all, even sand-sand get in own taste. But who dey satisfy with sand-sand? If they give you sand-sand to chop you go chop?

SILVA (*beginning to doubt his senses*). Mr Chume, if I tell you I understand one word of what you're saying I commit the sin of mendacity.

CHUME. What! You no know wetin pepper be? Captain Winston, as soon as I say pepper 'e know wetin I mean one time.

SILVA. I do not know, to use your own quaint expression, wetin musical pepper be, Mr Chume.

CHUME. And condiments? Iru? Salt? Ogiri? Kaun? And so on and so forth?

SILVA. Mr Chume, I'm afraid I don't quite see the relevance.

CHUME. No no, no try for *see* am. Make you just *hear* am. (*Blows a straight note.*) Dat na plain soup. (*Blows again, slurring into a higher note.*) Dat one na soup and pepper. (*Gives a new twist.*) Dat time I put extra flavour. Now, if you like we fit lef' am like that. But suppose I put stockfish, smoke-fish, ngwam-ngwam...

SILVA. If you don't mind I would just as soon have a straight-forward rehearsal. We have no time for all this nonsense.

CHUME. Wait small, you no like ngwam-ngwam or na wetin? Na my traditional food you dey call nonsense?

SILVA. I had no intention whatsoever to insult you, Mr Chume.

CHUME. If nonsense no to big insult for man of my calibre, den I no know wetin be insult again.

SILVA. Brother Chume, please. Do remember we have an important date at tomorrow's executions We must rehearse!

CHUME (*blasts an aggressive note on the trumpet*). Stockfish! (*Another.*) Bitter-leaf! I done tire for your nonsense. (*Throws down cap, blows more notes.*) Locust bean and red pepper! (*Kicks off shoes.*) If you still dey here when I put the ngwam-ngwam you go sorry for your head.

Throws himself into the music now, turning the tune into a traditional beat and warming up progressively. His legs begin to slice into the rhythm and before long his entire body is caught up with it. He dances aggressively towards SILVA *who backs away but cannot immediately escape as* CHUME's *dance controls the exit. Finally when* CHUME *leaps to one side he seizes his chance and takes to his heels.* CHUME *continues dancing and does not notice* BROTHER JERO *who enters and, after a despairing shake of his head, with his usual calculating gesture, steps into the dance with him.* CHUME *becomes slowly aware that other legs have joined his, his movement peters to a stop and he follows the legs up to the smiling, benevolent face of* BROTHER JERO. CHUME *backs off.*

JERO (*holds out his arms*). It is no ghost, Brother Chume. It is no apparition that stands before you. Assure yourself that you are well again and suffer no more from hallucinations. It is I, your old beloved master the Prophet Jeroboam. Immaculate Jero. Articulate Hero of Christ's Crusade.

CHUME (*he stands stock still*). Commot here before I break your head.

JERO. Break my head? What good will my broken head do you?

CHUME. It will make compensation for all de ting I done suffer for your hand. I dey warn you now, commot.

JERO. Suffer at my hands? You, Brother Chume? Suffer at my hands.

CHUME. You tell the police say I craze. Because God expose you and your cunny-cunny and I shout 'am for the whole world . . .

JERO. Brother Chume . . .

CHUME. I no be your Brother, no call me your brother. De kin' brother wey you fit be na the brotherhood of Cain and Abel. The brotherhood of Jacob and Esau. Eat my meat and tief my patrimony . . .

JERO. You do me great injustice, Brother Chume.

CHUME. Na so? And de one you do me na justice? To lock man

inside lunatic asylum because you wan' cover up your wayo. You be wayo man plain and simple. Wayo prophet! (*Warming up.*) Look, I dey warn you, commot here if you like your head! (*Advancing.*)

JERO. You raised your hand once against the anointed of the Lord, remember what it cost you.

CHUME. Which anointed of the Lord? You?

JERO. You raised a cutlass against me Brother Chume, but I forgave you.

CHUME. Dat na forgiveness? Three month inside lunatic asylum! Na dat den dey call forgiveness for your bible?

JERO. Was that not better than a life sentence for attempted murder?

CHUME. If to say I get my cutlass inside your head that time this world for done become better place. They can hang me but I for become saint and martyr. I for die but de whole world go call me Saint Chume.

JERO. But look round you, Brother Chume, look around you. You want to make this world a better place? Good! But to get hanged in the process? And perhaps in public? For whom? For the sake of people like Major Silva? People who don't even understand the musical soul which the Lord has given you? Are they worth it, Brother Chume? Oh I was watching you for some time you know – that man is an enemy believe me. An enemy. He does not understand you. I am sure they are all like that.

CHUME. They are not all like that. Captain Winston . . .

JERO. A white man. He is not one of us. And you know yourself he's a hypocrite. All white men are hypocrites.

CHUME. Na him come save me from that lunatic asylum, not so? If dat na hympocrisy then thank God for hympocrites.

JERO. He needed a trumpeter.

CHUME. Before that time I no fit play trumpet. I no sabbe hol' am self.

JERO. But you were playing on a penny flute and he heard you. I know the whole story, Brother Chume. He and his band came round to comfort you unfortunate inmates ...

CHUME (*violently*). I am not unfortunate inmate. Na you tell them to lock me inside dat place with crazemen. The day I fust meet you, dat day na my unfortunate.

JERO (*going progressively into a 'sermonic' chanting style*). Brother Chume, you should thank the good Lord, not blame him for the situation in which you found yourself. When he, in his wisdom saw fit to place wings on my feet and make me fly upon the deserted beach away from your flaming cutlass of wrath, it was not, be assured, my life upon which he set such value. No, Brother Chume, it was yours. Yours! Consider, if you had indeed achieved your nefarious intention and martyred me upon the sands, would not your soul be damned for ever? Picture my blood sinking into the sand and mingling with the foam, your feet sinking into the gruesome mixture and growing heavy with the knowledge of eternal damnation. What man, be he so swift of foot can run unaided upon a sandy shore? Could you think to escape the hounds of God's judgement and the law? See yourself as you would be, a fugitive from man and God, a dark soul lost and howling in the knowledge of damnation. Or would you fling yourself upon the waves and seek to drown yourself? If you succeeded, you were doubly damned. If you failed and the sea rejected you, flung your tainted body back upon the shore, think what a life of rejection yours would be, unable to seek solace even in death! Did you not yourself mention the moral tale of Cain and Abel only this minute? Was Cain not damned for ever? Was he not cursed by the Almighty himself? But I knew it was not in you to perform such an evil act. It was, obviously, the work of the devil. Your mind was turned away from the light of reason and your judgement clouded for a while. Was it then wrong of me to protect you the only way I could? For three months you received tender care and treatment. Your good woman, Amope, seeing her husband in danger of losing his reason proved once again that a heart of gold beat beneath her shrewish nature. For the first time since your marriage, Brother Chume, you saw that a voice of honey may lurk beneath the sandy tongue of a termagant. She showed you the care and love which she had denied you these many years. And so at last, seeing that you had recovered your reason, the good Lord sent unto you a deliverer just as he did deliver Nebuchadnessar of old from the horror of darkness and insanity. Oh, Brother Chume, Brother Chume, great is the Lord and full of kindness. Let us kneel down and praise his name. Praise the Lord, Brother Chume, praise the Lord. Praise the Lord for the gift of reason and the gift of life. Then praise him also for your coming promotion, yes, your coming promotion for this is the glad tidings of which I am the humble bearer.

CHUME (*hesitant*). Promotion?

JERO. Of whose glad tidings I am made humble bearer. I send *you*, Prophet Jero, said the Lord. Blessed are the peacemakers for they shall inherit the kingdom. Make your peace with Brother Chume and take with you this peace-offering, the good tidings of his coming promotion.

CHUME. Promotion? How can?

JERO (*sternly*). Do you doubt, Brother Chume? Do you doubt my prophecy? Has your sojourn among lunatics made you forget who prophesied war and have we not lived to see it come to pass? Do you trust in me and praise the Lord or do you confess yourself a waverer at this hour of trial.

CHUME. Praise the Lord.

JERO. In his new image, brother, sing his praise.

CHUME. Sing his praise.

JERO. Through blood has he purged us, as prophesied by me.

CHUME. Sing his praise.

JERO. Sing his praise, hallelujah, sing his praise.

CHUME. Hallelujah!

JERO. Out of the dark he brought you, into the light.

CHUME. Hallelujah!

JERO (*going all out to truly arouse* CHUME's *'rhythmic rapport'*).
Out of the dark he brought you, into the light!

CHUME. Hallelujah!

JERO. Never again to stumble, never again.

CHUME. Hallelujah!

JERO. Sent him off howling, praise Him, fire in his tail.

CHUME. Hallelujah!

JERO. Praise the Lord Hallelujah praise the Lord.

CHUME. Hallelujah!

JERO. Praise the Lord, Brother, praise the Lord.

CHUME. Praise the Lord, Brother, praise the Lord.

JERO. Praise the Lord, Brother, praise the Lord.

CHUME. Hallelujah! Hallelujah, praise the Lord, Hallelujah!
Praise the Lord. Hallelujah, praise the Lord, Hallelujah! Praise
the Lord . . .

With JERO *clapping in rhythm and* BROTHER CHUME *swaying
and chanting on his knees.*

JERO (*moves aside and detachedly observes* CHUME *in ecstasy*). I
had my doubts for a while but I should have known better.
These Salvation Army brothers may be washed in the red
blood of the Lord, but the black blood of the Bar Beach
brotherhood proves stronger every time. (*Sudden shout, turning
to* CHUME.) Hallelujah, Brother, Hallelujah!

He joins CHUME *for a few more moments, then taps him on the
shoulder.*

JERO. Brother Chume. Brother Chume. (*He shakes him a
little.*) Brother Chume. Brother Chume!

Picks up the trumpet and blows a blast in CHUME's *ear.*

CHUME (*starts out of his ecstasy*). Here, Brother Jero.

JERO (*with excitement*). The trumpet of the Lord, Chume! It sounds the clarion to duty. There is a time for everything, so says the Lord. A time for laughing and time for crying; a time for waking and a time for sleeping; a time for praying and a time for action. This is a time for action.

CHUME. Action?

JERO. Yes, action. Rise, Brother Chume, and follow me. The Lord hath need of thee.

CHUME (*getting up, hastily pulls himself together*). Of me, Brother Jero?

JERO. Yes, of you. You have stayed too long among the opposition. Cheated. Humiliated. Scorned. It is time for your elevation. Pick up your trumpet and follow me. I shall explain it all on our way to meet your – (*He pauses for deliberate emphasis.*) – Brother *Prophets.*

CHUME (*open-mouthed*). Brother Prophets, Brother Jero? But me na . . .

JERO. Not any longer, Chume. From now you are a holy prophet in your own light. No, no, that is *not* the promotion. It is only the first taste. Your full elevation takes place tonight, before the assembled brotherhood of the beach. You have gone through the fires of hell and emerged a strong servant of the Lord. You are saved, redeemed, inspired and re-dedicated. From now on, a true brother, an equal; no longer a servant of mine. Kneel, Brother Chume.

CHUME (*kneeling groggily*). But prophet . . . me na only poor . . .

JERO. I perform only the good Lord's commands, nothing more. (*With his holy rod he taps him on both shoulders.*) Arise Prophet Chume, serve the Lord and fight his cause till eternity. (*Turns the rod round and offers him the 'hilt'.*) Until you obtain yours and it is consecrated you may use mine.

CHUME (*overwhelmed*). Dis kindness too much, Brother Jero.

JERO. I am only the instrument of the Lord's will. (*Briskly.*) Now get up and let's go. The others are awaiting and we have much to do.

Blackout.

SCENE THREE

The front space of BROTHER JERO'S *headquarters. Loud chatter among a most bizarre collection of prophets.* SISTER REBECCA *emerges from the house carrying the portrait from the office and hangs it against the outer wall. The desk and chair have already been moved out of the office for the meeting. Rebecca takes a chair to a most unbending individual who stares straight ahead and keeps his arms folded. He is the only one who seems to abstain from the free-flowing drinks, the effect of which is already apparent on one or two.*

SHADRACH. No, Sister, we refuse to sit down. We refuse to sit down. We have been slighted and we make known our protest. We have been treated with less courtesy than becomes the leader of a denomination twenty thousand strong. Brother Jero, at whose behest we have presented ourselves here at great inconvenience, is not himself here to welcome us. We protest his discourtesy.

CALEB. Hear hear. (*Hiccups.*) Hardly the conduct of a gentleman prophet.

REBECCA. Brother Shadrach, I assure you he was held up by matters which concern this very affair you have come to discuss.

ISAAC. He is very long about it then.

SHADRACH. Much much too long, Sister Rebecca. To make us wait is an act of indignity thrust upon us.

ANANAIAS. Oh sit down, you fatuous old hypocrite.

SHADRACH (*turns to go*). We take our leave.

CALEB. Hear hear. (*Hiccup.*) Let's all stage a dignified walk-out. Nobody walks out these days. Not since the parliamentarians vanished.

ISAAC. Good old days those. Good for the profession.

CALEB. Come on, old Shad, give us a walk-out. (*With much difficulty on the word.*) An ecclesiastically dignified walk-out.

REBECCA. Brother Shadrach, please . . .

SHADRACH. No, we take our leave. For the third time tonight we have been insulted by a common riff-raff of the calling. We take our leave.

CALEB. Hear hear. The honourable member for . . .

REBECCA. Pay no attention Brother. I apologize on their behalf. Forgive us all for being remiss.

SHADRACH. I forgive you, Sister. (*Sits down.*)

ANANAIAS (*leans over the back of his chair*). You will burst, Shadrach, you will burst like the frog in the swamp.

CALEB. Like the frog in the adage, Brother. (*Hiccup.*) Frog in the adage.

SHADRACH (*without losing his poise, whips his hand round and seizes that of* ANANAIAS *by the wrist and brings it round front. The hand is seen to contain a purse*). Mine, I believe, Ananaias?

ANANAIAS. It dropped on the ground. Is that the thanks I get for helping you pick it up.

SHADRACH. I accuse no one, Ananaias. (*Returning wallet into the recesses of his robes.*) We are all met, I hope, in a spirit of brotherhood. The lesson reads, I am my brother's keeper Ananaias, not, I am my brother's pursekeeper.

ANANAIAS (*turns away*). Lay not your treasures upon earth says the good book. Verily verily I say unto you, it is easier for a camel and so on and so forth.

CALEB (*raising his mug*). Sister Rebecca, my spirits are low.

REBECCA (*rushing to fill it*). Forgive me, Brother Caleb.

CALEB. Upliftment is in order, God bless you.

ISAAC. So where is this Jeroboam fellow? When is he coming to tell us why he has made us forsake our stations to wait on his lordship?

REBECCA. In a moment, Brother Matthew. (*Going to fill his mug.*)

ISAAC. I am not Brother Matthew . . .

REBECCA. I beg your pardon, Brother.

CALEB. A clear case of mistaken identity, Sister Rebecca.

ISAAC. I am not Brother Matthew, sister, and I beg you to note that fact.

MATTHEW (*nettled*). May one ask just what you have against being Brother Matthew?

ISAAC. I know all about Brother Matthew, and that should be enough answer for anyone with a sense of shame.

REBECCA. Forgive my unfortunate error. Don't start a quarrel on that account.

ISAAC. And to think he has the nerve to show his face here. Some people are utterly without shame.

CALEB. Hear hear.

MATTHEW. And others are poor imitation Pharisees.

CALEB. Hear hear.

ISAAC. Better an imitation Pharisee than a sex maniac.

MATTHEW. I take exception to that!

ISAAC. Very good. Take exception.

MATTHEW. Dare repeat that and see if it doesn't land you in court for slander. Go on, we are all listening. I have witnesses. Come on I dare you.

ISAAC. I don't have to. We all know the truth. You may have been acquitted but we know the truth.

MATTHEW. Coward!

ISAAC. Fornicator.

MATTHEW. Drunkard, con-man. Forger.

CALEB. Three to one. Foul play.

REBECCA (*getting between them as they head for a clash*). Brothers, in the name of our common calling I beg of you . . .

JERO *and* CHUME *enter.* REBECCA *sighs with relief.*

Oh, Brother Jero, you are truly an answer to prayer.

JERO. Welcome, Brothers, welcome all of you and forgive me for arriving late at my own meeting. (*Hands* REBECCA *a key.*) Unlock the safe and bring out our secret weapon, Sister.

ISAAC. We have waited two hours, Brother.

ANANAIAS. You have not been here a half-hour Isaac. I saw you come in.

JERO. A-ah, I see empty mugs. No wonder our brothers are offended. Sister Rebecca, we require better hospitality.

REBECCA (*emerging with the file*). Do you think that wise, Brother Jero? They are already quite . . .

JERO. Trust me, I know what I am doing Sister. (*Loudly.*) More drinks for our brothers. Fill up the cups Sister Rebecca.

SHADRACH. We do not drink. We came here for a serious discussion, so we were informed. We have not come here to wine and dine.

JERO. We will not quarrel. I admit the fault is mine. Sister Rebecca, some snuff for Brother Shadrach.

REBECCA. I shall get it at once, Brother Jero.

JERO (*turns and beams on the gathering*). And now, dear brother shepherds of the flock, let us waste no more time. We are mostly known to one another so I shall not waste your time on introductions. The subject is progress. Progress has caught up with us. Like the oceantide it is battering on our shore-line, the door-step of our tabernacle. Projects everywhere! Fun fairs! Gambling! Casinos! The servants of Mammon have had their heads turned by those foreign fleshpots to which they are drawn whenever they travel on their so-called economic missions. And our mission, the mission of the good Lord Jehovah shall be the sacrificial lamb, on the altar of Mammon. Oh when you see smoke rising on that grievous day, know that it rises from these shacks of devotion which we have raised to shelter the son of God on his Visitation on that long-awaited day. And shall he find? What shall he find when he comes over the water, that great fisherman among men, thinking to step on to the open tabernacle which we, you and I, have founded here to await his glorious coming? *THIS!* (*With a flourish he pulls out a sheaf of photographs from his bag.*) This, my brothers!

> JERO *observes their reactions as the photos of luscious scantily-clad bathers are circulated. Reactions vary from* SHADRACH *who turns away in calculated disgust to* ANANAIAS *who finds them lewdly hilarious and* MATTHEW *who literally drools.*

SHADRACH. It must never happen here!

ISAAC. Never. We must organize.

CALEB. I concur. Rally the union. No business sharks in our spirituous waters.

ISAAC. All legitimate avenues of protest must be explored.

MATTHEW. What for?

ANANAIAS. What do you mean, what for?

MATTHEW. I said what for? These photos reveal strayed souls in need of salvation. Must we turn away from suchlike? Only the sick have need of the physician.

ISAAC. Not your kind of physic, Brother Matthew.

SHADRACH. If we take Brother Jeroboam's meaning correctly, and we think we do, the intention is to exclude ... er ... us, the physicians from this so-called resort is it not, Brother?

MATTHEW. We don't know that for certain.

JERO (*hands him the file at an open page*). Read this, Brother Matthew. These are the minutes of the meeting of Cabinet at which certain decisions were taken.

MATTHEW (*shrinks away*). What file is that?

JERO. Read it.

MATTHEW. It says Confidential on that paper. I don't want any government trouble.

ISAAC. Very wise of you, Brother Matthew. Mustn't risk your parole. (*Takes the file.*) I'll read it. (*At the first glance he whistles.*) How did you get hold of this, Jero?

JERO. The Lord moves in mysterious ways . . .

ANANAIAS. . . . . His wonders to perform. Amen.

ISAAC (*reading*). 'Memorandum of the Cabinet Office to the Board of Tourism. Proposals to turn the Bar Beach into an a National Public Execution Amphitheatre.' Whew! You hadn't mentioned that.

JERO. I was saving it for a surprise. It is the heart of the whole business enterprise.

SHADRACH. We don't understand. Does this mean . . .?

JERO. Business, Brother Shadrach, big business.

MATTHEW. Where do we come in in all this?

JERO. Patience, we're coming to it. Brother Isaac, do read on. Go down to the section titled Slum Clearance.

ISAAC (*his expression clouds in fury*). Hn? Hn? Hng!!!

MATTHEW. What is it? What is it?

ISAAC. Riff-raff! They call us riff-raff!

JERO. Read it out, Brother Isaac.

ISAAC. 'Unfortunately the beach is at present cluttered up with riff-raff of all sorts who dupe the citizenry and make the beach unattractive to decent and respectable people. Chiefest among these are the so-called . . .' Oh may the wrath of Jehovah smite them on their blasphemous mouths!

JERO (*taking back the file*). Time is short, Brothers. We cannot afford to be over-sensitive. (*Reads.*) '. . . the so-called prophets and evangelists. All these are not only to be immediately expelled but steps must be taken to ensure that they never at any time find their way back to the execution stadium.'

SHADRACH. Fire and brimstone! Sodom and Gomorrah!

JERO. Patience Brothers, patience. 'It is proposed however, that since the purpose of public execution is for the moral edification and spiritual upliftment of the people, one respectable religious denomination be licensed to operate on the Bar Beach. Such a body will say prayers before and after each execution, and where appropriate will administer the last rites to the condemned. They will be provided a point of vantage where they will preach to the public on the evil of crime and the morals to be drawn from the miserable end of the felons. After which their brass band shall provide religious music.'

ISAAC. A brass band? That means . . .

JERO. Yes, the Salvation Army.

SHADRACH. Enough. We have heard all we need to know of the conspiracy against us. The question now is, what do we do to foil them?

JERO. Organize. Band together. Brother Matthew is right: the sick have need of healing. We must not desert the iniquitous in their greatest hour of need.

SHADRACH (*looking towards* CALEB, *then* ANANAIAS). We foresee problems in banding together with certain members of the calling.

JERO. All problems can be overcome. The stakes are high, Brother Shadrach.

SHADRACH. The price is also high.

ANANAIAS. Oh shut up, you fatuous hypocrite!

SHADRACH. Ananaias!

JERO. Peace, Brothers, peace. Ananaias, I shall require greater decorum from you.

ANANAIAS. You have it before you ask, Brother Jero. Anything you say.

MATTHEW. What does Jeroboam have in mind, exactly? You didn't call us together without some idea in your head.

JERO. Quite correct, Brother Matthew. I have outlined certain plans of action and have even begun to pursue them. The time is short, in fact, the moment is now upon us. The Bar Beach becomes the single execution arena, the sole amphitheatre of

death in the entire nation. Where at the moment we have
spectators in thousands, the proposed stadium will seat hun-
dreds of thousands. We must acquire the spiritual monopoly of
such a captive congregation.

CALEB. Hear, hear!

ISAAC (*impatiently*). Yes, but how?

JERO. We form ONE body. Acquire a new image. Let the actuality
of power see itself reflected in that image, reflected and comple-
mented. We shall prophesy with one voice, not as lone voices
crying in the wilderness, but as the united oracle of the spiritual
profession.

CALEB. Brother Jero, I hand it to you. I couldn't have phrased it
better and I pride myself on being a bookish sort of fellow.

MATTHEW. What image then?

JERO. Such an image as will make our outward colours one with
theirs.

CALEB. Show them up in their true colours you mean. (*He
splutters with laughter until he is coughing helplessly, near-
choking.*)

JERO. Brother Caleb, I think that remark was in very bad
taste.

MATTHEW (*wildly*). And dangerous. Very dangerous. I refuse to
remain one moment longer if such remarks are permitted. We
are not here to look for trouble. I dissociate myself from that
remark.

ISAAC. Still watching your parole, Brother Matthew?

CALEB (*leans over drunkenly*). Psst. Is it true the magistrate was a
sideman in your church?

JERO. Brothers, Brothers, this is no time for our private little
quarrels. We must not envy Brother Matthew his spiritual
influence in er . . . certain fortunate quarters when we are on
the threshold of bringing the highest and the mightiest under
our spiritual guidance.

SHADRACH. Are you day-dreaming? In a day or two you will not
even have a roof over your head and you speak of . . .

JERO. Yes Brother Shad, the highest and mightiest, I assure you, will come under our spiritual guidance.

SHADRACH. Success has swelled your head, Brother Jero.

CALEB. That's why he thinks big. (*Roars off alone into laughter.*)

JERO. Suppose I tell you, Shadrach, that it has come to the ears of the rulers that a certain new-formed religious body has prophesied a long life to the regime? That this mysterious body has declared that the Lord is so pleased with their er . . . spectacular efforts to stamp out armed robbery, with the speed of the trials, the refusal of the right to appeal, the rejection of silly legal technicalities and the high rate of executions, that all these things are so pleasing to the Lord that he has granted eternal life to their regime?

SHADRACH. They won't believe you.

JERO. They have already. The seed was well planted and it has taken root. Tomorrow the Tourist Board shall propose a certain religious body for the new amphitheatre. The Cabinet will be informed that it is the same body which has made the prophecy. Our spiritual monopoly shall be approved without debate – Does anyone doubt me?

SHADRACH. The Shadrach-Medrach-Abednego Apostolic Trinity has a twenty-thousand strong congregation all over the country. These include men from all walks of life including very high ranks within the uniformed profession. We propose therefore that our Apostolic Trinity absorb all other denominations into its spiritual bosom. . .

The proposal is greeted with instant howls of rejection.

JERO. No, Brother Shadrach. As you see, it just will not do. Are there any other proposals?

They all shrug at one another.

ISAAC. All right Jero, let's have your proposal.

JERO. You all know Brother Chume. Prophet Chume I ought to say.

MATTHEW. But he's the one who went off his head.

ANANAIAS. Looks saner than you or me. Cleaner anyway.

JERO. Prophet Chume has left the ranks of the enemy and cast his lot among us. With his help, with the intimate knowledge which he has acquired of the workings of that foreign body to which he once belonged we shall recreate ourselves in the required image. We shall manifest our united spiritual essence in the very form and shape of the rulers of the land. Nothing, you will agree could be more respectable than that. (*Rises*.) Sister Rebecca, bring out the banner!

REBECCA (*runs out with the flag, flushed with excitement*). Is this the moment, Brother Jero?

JERO. The moment is now, Sister. Witness now the birth of the first Church of the Apostolic Salvation Army of the Lord!

> CHUME *begins the tune of 'Are you washed in the Blood of the Lamb'*. REBECCA *sings lustily, deaf to the world*.

Behold the new body of the Lord! Forward into battle, Brothers!

ISAAC. Against what?

JERO. Precisely.

SHADRACH (*disdainfully*). Precisely what? He asks, against what? You say, precisely.

JERO. Precisely. Against what? We don't know any more than our secular models. They await a miracle, we will provide it.

SHADRACH (*indicating* CHUME). With lunatics like him. You fancy yourself an empire-builder.

JERO. A spiritual empire builder, Brother Shadrach. Those who are not with us, are against us. This is the Salvation Army with a difference. With pepper and ogiri. With ngwam-ngwan. Right, Brother Chume?

> CHUME *nods vigorously without stopping the music*.

ISAAC. Hey, you haven't said who is to be head of this Army.

CALEB. Good point. Very good point.

JERO. We come in as equals. We form a syndicate.

SHADRACH. Everybody needs a head.

CALEB (*solemnly*). Old Shad is de-ee-eep. (*Hiccups.*)

JERO. A titular head. He gives the orders and keeps close watch on the church treasury. Purely ceremonial.

ISAAC. Yes, but who? Who do you have in mind for Captain?

JERO. Captain, Brother Isaac? No, no, not captain. We must not cut our image small in the eyes of the world. General, at least.

SHADRACH. And who would that be, you still haven't said.

JERO. Whoever has the secrets of the Tourist Board in his hands. Whoever can guarantee that the new body does obtain nomination from the Tourist Board.

ANANAIAS. I knew it. I knew he was keeping something to himself.

ISAAC. You have thought of everything, haven't you?

JERO. You may say I am divinely inspired, Brother Isaac.

SHADRACH. And you, we presume, are in possession of the aforesaid secrets?

JERO. Have we a united body or not?

ANANAIAS. Christ! Those fat pockets begging to be picked while their owners are laughing at the poor devil at the stake. It's a sin to be missing from this garden of Eden. (*Throws* JERO *a salute.*) General! Reporting for duty, sir.

JERO (*saluting in turn*). Sergeant-major! Go in the room and find a uniform that fits you.

ISAAC. Millionaire businessmen! Expensive sinners coming to enjoy the Bar Beach show.

JERO. Who else is for the Army of the Lord?

ISAAC. It's Sodom and Gomorrah. The milk is sour and the honey is foul.

JERO. Who is for the Army of the Lord?

ISAAC. What rank do you have in mind for me?

JERO. Major. (*Gestures.*) In there. You'll find a uniform that fits you.

> *As he goes in* ANANAIAS *returns singing lustily and banging a tambourine. He is uniformed in what looks like a Salvation Army outfit except for the cap which is the 'indigenous' touch, made in local material and 'abetiaja' style. The combination is ludicrous.*

MATTHEW (*takes another look at the picture of a curvaceous bathing belle and decides*). I used to play the flute a little, Brother Jer . . . I mean General Jeroboam. In fact I was once in my school band.

JERO. You'll find a uniform in there, Captain.

SHADRACH. The uniform will not change you. You will still be the same Bar Beach riff-raff no matter what you wear. Nobody will give you a monopoly.

CALEB. Wrong on all counts, Brother Shad. By the cut of his tailor shall a man be known. Uniform maketh man.

JERO. Very soon the syndicate will be closed. The Army hierarchy is for foundation members only. We hold office by divine grace, in perpetuity. Join now or quit.

SHADRACH. Overreacher. We know your kind, Jeroboam. Continue to count your chickens.

CALEB. Wrong again, Shad. You don't know the worthy Jero it seems. If he says he'll get the monopoly, he will. A thorough methodical man, very much after my heart.

JERO. What rank do you want, Caleb?

CALEB. I'll stick out for Colonel. I may be slightly (*Hiccups.*) see what I mean, but I know what's what. I'm an educated man and that's a rare commodity in this outfit. Present company naturally excepted, General.

JERO. Lieutenant-Colonel.

CALEB. General, I'm thinking that instead of merely preaching at the assembly we could do a morality play, you know, something like our Easter and Christmas Cantata. I'm quite nifty at things like that – The Rewards of Sin, The Terrible End of the Desperado . . . and so on. Well er . . . that sort of specialized duties deserves a higher rank don't you think, mon General?

JERO (*firmly*). Lieutenant - Colonel.

CALEB (*throws a drunken salute*). So be it, mon General.

Goes in. The others are coming out, uniformed.

JERO. You are alone, Shadrach.

SHADRACH. We are never alone. We proceed this minute to the Chairman of the Tourist Board, there to put an end to our ambitions. The much-respected aunt of the Chairman is a devout member of our flock.

JERO (*looks at his watch*). If you wish to see the Chief Executive Officer in person he will arrive in a few minutes. He was invited to this meeting.

SHADRACH. Here?

JERO. He will negotiate for the other side.

SHADRACH. Bluff! The only officer you'll see here is the Eviction Officer.

ANANAIAS (*looking out*). My General, the enemy is without!

JERO. Let him pass freely.

ANANAIAS. What do they want? (*Going to the door.*) You're back are you? Lucky for you the General gives you safe conduct.

EXECUTIVE. You have a nerve summoning us here at this time of night. (*Blocking his ears.*) Will you tell them to stop that lunatic din!

JERO. Colonel Chume . . .

ANANAIAS. He won't hear. I'll stop him for you.

Goes over, salutes and takes the trumpet from his mouth.

JERO. Sit down.

EXECUTIVE. I demand . . .
JERO. Seat him down Sergeant-Major.
ANANAIAS. My pleasure, General, sir.

> *Forces down the* CHIEF EXECUTIVE *into a chair. The* CLERK *quickly scurries into a seat.*

JERO. Excuse me while I get ready for the negotiations.

> *He picks the file off the table with deliberate movements. The* EXECUTIVE OFFICER *stares at the file fascinated. He exchanges looks with the* CLERK *who quickly looks down.*
> JERO *goes into the room.*

SHADRACH. We are, we presume, in the presence of the Chief Eviction Officer of the Tourist Board.
CLERK. No, that's C.E.O. II. This is C.E.O. I, Chief Executive Officer. C.E.O. III is still to be appointed – that's the Chief Execution Officer, a new post.
EXECUTIVE (*turns to inspect* SHADRACH *slowly, like a strange insect*). And who might you be?
SHADRACH. Leader of the Shadrach-Medrach-Abednego Apostolic flock, twenty thousand strong.
EXECUTIVE (*wearily*). Another fanatic.
SHADRACH. It is our hope that you have come here to put an end to the schemes of this rapacious trader on piety who calls himself . . .
EXECUTIVE. Oh Christ!

> *Enter* JERO, *resplendent in a Salvation Army General uniform.* CHUME *blares a fanfare on the trumpet.*

JERO. The file, Sister Rebecca.
EXECUTIVE. And now I hope you will . . .
JERO. You came, I trust, alone as requested.

EXECUTIVE. Yes I foolishly risked my life coming without protection to this haunt of cut-throats.

JERO. It was entirely in your own interests.

EXECUTIVE. So you said. And now perhaps you will kindly tell me what my interests are.

JERO. They are such as might be unsuitable for the ears of a policeman. That is why I suggested that you leave your escort behind.

EXECUTIVE. Come to the point.

JERO (*takes a seat, carefully brushing his creases*). You will remember that when the Chief Eviction Officer was compelled, as a result of the violent spiritual conversion of Colonel Rebecca . . .

EXECUTIVE. Colonel who?

JERO. Colonel Rebecca of the Church of the Apostolic Salvation Army. CASA for short. Do you know that Casa means home? In this case, spiritual home. I am sure you approve our new image.

Enter REBECCA *with file. She is now in uniform.*

EXECUTIVE. Your image does not interest me in the slightest.

JERO. And your own image Chief Executive Officer?

Hands him two sheets of paper from the file.

Great is the Lord and Mighty in his ways. He led your Chief Eviction Officer to my door in the company of one He had marked down for salvation, overwhelmed him with the onslaught of such hot holiness that he fled leaving his documents in the possession of a woman possessed.

EXECUTIVE. What do you want? Just say what you want?

JERO. Monopoly is the subject of your file No. I.B.P. stroke 537 stroke 72A. Beauty parlours, supermarkets, restaurants, cafés and ice-cream kiosks, fair-grounds, construction and hiring of beach huts, amusement gadgets, gambling machines and dodgems and roundabouts and parking facilities – for the new National Amphitheatre to be built on the Bar Beach. Mr Executive Officer, the list is endless, but what is of interest to the good Lord whose interests I represent is the method of awarding these very superabundant contracts.

EXECUTIVE. No need to talk so loud. (*Looks round nervously.*) Just say what you want.

JERO. Render unto Caesar what is Caesar's, and unto God what is God's.

EXECUTIVE. What does that mean in plain Caesar's language?

JERO. A monopoly on spirituality.

EXECUTIVE. What's that?

JERO. Made out to the Church of the Apostolic Salvation Army. CASA.

SHADRACH. We on this side place our trust in your integrity not to accede to any such request.

EXECUTIVE. Will someone tell me who this fellow is?

JERO. Colonel Rebecca has been kind enough to prepare the letter. It requires only your signature she tells me.

EXECUTIVE (*taking the letter, incredulous*). Is that all? Just a monopoly on the rights to hold religious rallies here?

JERO. It's enough.

EXECUTIVE. Not even a monopoly on some small business enterprise?

JERO. We are already in business. Of course we expect you to declare that all land actually occupied as of now by the various religious bodies would from now on be held in trust, managed and developed by the newly approved representative body of all apostolic bodies, CASA. . .

EXECUTIVE. What!

SHADRACH. Mr Executive Officer . . .

EXECUTIVE. What has that to do with monopoly on spirituality?

JERO. Spirituality, to take root, must have land to take root in.

EXECUTIVE. Yes, yes, of course, I – er – see your point.

JERO. Our image also conforms on all levels. We are not fanatics.

Our symbol is blood. It washes all sins away. *All* sins, Mr Tourist Board.

EXECUTIVE. Yes, indeed. A point decidedly in your favour.

SHADRACH. We protest, sir. We strongly protest!

EXECUTIVE. Who is this man?

JERO. An apostate. Ignore him. (SHADRACH *splutters speechlessly.* JERO *pushes a piece of paper to the official.*) The declaration. It says nothing but the truth You are present at the meeting for apostolic union. You see yourself the new body which has emerged, fully representative.

SHADRACH. Thieves! Robbers! Rapists and cut-throats!

JERO. We did not include you, Brother Shadrach.

> The EXECUTIVE OFFICER *signs, then* JERO *pushes it to the* CLERK.

Witness it. (*The* CLERK *looks at* EXECUTIVE OFFICER.)

EXECUTIVE. Sign the damn thing and let's get out of here.

JERO (*hands the paper to* REBECCA). Are those their genuine signatures, Colonel?

EXECUTIVE (*offended*). I don't double-deal. I am a man of my word.

JERO. It isn't that I don't trust you.

REBECCA. It is their signatures, my General.

EXECUTIVE. And now may I have ...

JERO. Your list of contracts? Just one more paper to be signed. The attachment. The survey map which indicates what portions of the beach are referred to as trust property of CASA.

EXECUTIVE. This is impossible. We have allocated some of the land squatted on by your ...

JERO. Please give me the credit of having done my home-work. You forget we have had a formidable ally in the person of Colonel Rebecca, your former Confidential Secretary. And we have drawn on that precious file which your Eviction Officer so generously loaned us. There is no duplication, check it if you wish.

EXECUTIVE. All right, all right. (*About to sign.*)

SHADRACH. Don't sign your soul away to the devil, sir!

EXECUTIVE. Can't you shut him up?

JERO. Sergeant-major!

ANANAIAS. My pleasure sir. Come on, Shad.

Holds him expertly by the elbow and ejects him.

SHADRACH. We protest most strenuously at this barefaced conspiracy. We shall pursue it to the highest level. The leader of a flock twenty thousand strong is not to be taken lightly we promise you . . .

EXECUTIVE. Are you sure he won't make trouble later? (*He signs.*)

JERO. Leave him to us. The testimony of the Salvation Army will weigh against that of a disgruntled charlatan anywhere. (*Takes the map and returns the incriminating papers.*) Your documents, sir. I hope you take better care of them next time.

EXECUTIVE (*grabs them quickly, glances through and stuffs them in his pockets*). And now to go and deal with that stupid Eviction Officer.

JERO. Blame him not. The power of the spirit on murky souls overcomes the strictest civil service discipline.

EXECUTIVE. Don't preach at me, humbug.

JERO. On the contrary we will preach at you. Every Tuesday at twelve o'clock the Church of Apostolic Salvation Army will preach outside your office. The subject of our sermons shall be, the evils of corruption – of the soul. We intend to restrict ourselves to spiritual matters. We will not contradict the secular image.

The CLERK bursts out laughing. The EXECUTIVE eyes him balefully and the laughter dries on his face.

EXECUTIVE. You report to me in my office first thing tomorrow morning. You and the Eviction Officer. (*Storms out.*)

ANANAIAS (*as the* CHIEF CLERK *hesitates*). Hey you, follow your master.

CLERK. Er . . . Brother . . . I mean . . . er – General, you wouldn't . . . I mean . . . by any chance . . . what I mean to say is . . . even a Lance-Corporal would do me.

REBECCA. Glory be! (*Rushes forward to embrace him.*) I think there is a uniform just his size, my General.

JERO. As you wish Colonel, Lance-Corporal it is then.

ANANAIAS. What next, my General?

JERO. No time like the present. We march this moment and show the flag. Brother Chume, kneel for your second christening. Or third. I'm beginning to lose count. (CHUME *kneels.* JERO *anoints his head.*) Go down, Brother Chume, rise Brigadier Joshua!

SEVERALLY (*amidst embraces*). God bless you, Joshua. God bless Brigadier Joshua.

CHUME (*overwhelmed*). Oh Brother – sorry General – Jero. I am so unworthy . . .

JERO. Nonsense, Chume, you are the very ornament of your rank. Stand to action Brigade. Brigadier Joshua will lead, blowing the trumpet. Sergeant Ananaias!

ANANAIAS. My General?

JERO. When Joshua blows the trumpet, it will be your duty to make the miracle happen. The walls shall come tumbling down or you will have some explaining to do.

ANANAIAS. Leave it to me, my General.

JERO. Just lean on the rotting walls Ananaias and the Lord will do the rest. By dawn the entire beach must be cleansed of all pestilential separatist shacks which infest the holy atmosphere of the united apostolate of the Lord. Beginning naturally with Apostate Shadrach's unholy den. The fire and the sword, Ananaias, the fire and the sword. Light up the night of evil with the flames of holiness! Consecrate the grounds for the Bar Beach Spectacular!

ANANAIAS. Apostolic Army of the Lord, Atten . . . tion! Forward, Banner of the Lord! (REBECCA *takes up position.*) Forward, Trumpet of the Lord! (CHUME *positions himself.*) Sound the Trumpet! By the left, Quick . . . Swing against Corrup . . . tion!

> CHUME *blasts the first bar of 'Joshua Fit the Battle of Jericho' in strict tempo, then swings elated into a brisk indigenous rhythm to which the Army march–dance out into the night.* JERO, *with maximum condescension acknowledges the salute of the army. As the last man disappears, he takes a last look at the framed photo, takes it down and places it face towards the wall, takes from a drawer in the table an even larger photo of himself in his present uniform and mounts it on the wall. He then seats himself at the table and pulls towards him a file or two, as if to start work. Looks up suddenly and on his face is the amiable-charlatan grin.*

JERO. After all, it is the fashion these days to be a desk General.

Blackout.

THE END

Methuen's Modern Plays

David Edgar	*Destiny*
	Mary Barnes
Michael Frayn	*Clouds*
	Alphabetical Order and *Donkeys' Years*
	Make and Break
Max Frisch	*The Fire Raisers*
	Andorra
Simon Gray	*Butley*
	Otherwise Engaged and other plays
	Dog Days
	The Rear Column and other plays
	Close of Play and *Pig in a Poke*
	Stage Struck
Peter Handke	*Offending the Audience* and *Self-Accusation*
	Kaspar
	The Ride Across Lake Constance
	They Are Dying Out
Barrie Keeffe	*Gimme Shelter (Gem, Gotcha, Getaway)*
	Barbarians (Killing Time, Abide With Me, In the City)
	A Mad World, My Masters
Arthur Kopit	*Indians*
	Wings
David Mercer	*After Haggerty*
	The Bankrupt and other plays
	Cousin Vladimir & Shooting the Chandelier
	Duck Song
	Huggy Bear and other plays
	The Monster of Karlovy Vary & Then and Now
	No Limits to Love
John Mortimer	*Collaborators*
	Come as You Are
Peter Nichols	*Passion Play*
Joe Orton	*Loot*
	What the Butler Saw
	Funeral Games and *The Good and Faithful Servant*
	Entertaining Mr Sloane
	Up Against It
Harold Pinter	*The Birthday Party*
	The Room and *The Dumb Waiter*
	The Caretaker
	A Slight Ache and other plays
	The Collection and *The Lover*
	The Homecoming
	Tea Party and other plays
	Landscape and *Silence*
	Old Times
	No Man's Land
	Betrayal
	The Hothouse
Luigi Pirandello	*Henry IV*
	Six Characters in Search of an Author
Stephen Poliakoff	*Hitting Town* and *City Sugar*

If you would like regular information on new Methuen plays and theatre books, please write to:

The Marketing Department
Eyre Methuen Ltd
North Way
Andover
Hants